PROGRAM IMPLEMENTATION

CONTEMPORARY EVALUATION RESEARCH
A series of books on applied social science

Series Editors:
HOWARD E. FREEMAN, *Institute for Social Science Research, UCLA*
RICHARD A. BERK, *Department of Sociology, University of California, Santa Barbara*

The CONTEMPORARY EVALUATION RESEARCH series meets the need for a monograph-length publication outlet for timely manuscripts on evaluation research. In the tradition of EVALUATION REVIEW (formerly EVALUATION QUARTERLY), studies from different disciplines and methodological perspectives will be included. The series will cover the full spectrum of substantive areas, including medical care, mental health, criminal justice, manpower, income security, education and the environment. Manuscripts may report empirical results, methodological developments or review an existing literature.

The Series Editors and Publishers are grateful to the Editorial Board of EVALUATION REVIEW for assistance in the external manuscript review process of this series.

PROGRAM IMPLEMENTATION

The Organizational Context

MARY ANN SCHEIRER

CONTEMPORARY EVALUATION RESEARCH
A series of books on applied social science edited by
HOWARD E. FREEMAN and **RICHARD A. BERK**   5

 **SAGE** PUBLICATIONS Beverly Hills London

For information address:

SAGE Publications, Inc.   SAGE Publications Ltd
275 South Beverly Drive   28 Banner Street
Beverly Hills, California 90212   London EC1Y 8QE, England

Printed in the United States of America

Library of Congress Cataloging in Publication Data

Scheirer, Mary Ann.
  Program implementation.

  (Contemporary evaluation research ; v. 5)
  Originally presented as the author's thesis
(Ph.D.--Cornell University)
  Bibliography: p.
  1. Social work administration--United States.
I. Title. II. Series.
HV91.S286   1981   361.3'068   81-689
ISBN 0-8039-1540-3   AACR2

FIRST PRINTING

Contents

List of Appendices

List of Tables and Figures

Acknowledgments

The conception and implementation of the research reported in this book benefited greatly from the unfailing support and good advice of my doctoral committee chairman at Cornell University, Robin M. Williams, Jr. Other committee members, Henry Alker and Karl Weick, provided many valuable suggestions and stimulating critiques. My work on this research was supported by a social psychology traineeship from the National Institute of General Medical Sciences, Grant Number 5T01GM01941-09.

This research was also made possible by the cooperation extended by the many anonymous staff members of the Developmental Center and the Psychiatric Center, whose willingness to be interviewed made data collection feasible. Particular thanks are due to Chief Psychologists William Connor and Nurhan Findikyan for their great help in facilitating understanding of the programs as well as opening doors to other staff of their organizations. In addition, I am grateful for permission granted by Dr. Findikyan to reproduce the Goal Plan Form, shown in the Appendices.

Interviewers who greatly assisted the data collection process were Robert Infurna and Elissa Savrin. Able assistance with record coding was provided by Connie Caroli and Karen Piatt. The several versions of this manuscript would not have been produced without the excellent typing of Joan Thiele, Ann Nawaz, Rohini Dhanda-McMillan and Karla Larkin.

Finally, my greatest debt must be to C. James Scheirer, whose constant support, encouragement, constructive critiques, and cooking skills have energized this project from the beginning. Last, but never least, Eric and Laura provided distraction and renewal when the effort of writing threatened to become overwhelming. To their generation this book is dedicated.

—Mary Ann Scheirer

Series Editors' Introduction

Regardless of program area, thoughtful and rigorous evaluations often reveal a lack of efficacy and efficiency of intervention efforts. Program sponsors and managers naturally enough try to blame the evaluation studies, many of which are undeniably either avoidably or unavoidably flawed. Equally understandable is the reaction of evaluators, who explain their results in terms of a lack of boldness of programs they have evaluated. Again, this justification for negative findings sometimes may be relevant. But neither explanation is sufficient; there are both sound evaluation studies and creative interventions. Increasingly, then, a third possibility needs to be reckoned with—program failures frequently are a result of faulty implementation.

The notion that often programs are not implemented well is hardly new. But the several decades of relatively systematic assessment of efforts to improve social and human conditions without too many notable successes, and the increasingly constrained resources available, have directed attention to the problems, difficulties, and pitfalls that are found in planning and undertaking interventions in the health, education, and human service fields. Program implementation is emerging as the focal point of attention in our efforts to maximize the benefits to be derived from public and private expenditures for local, national, and international intervention efforts. Thus, Mary Ann Scheirer's monograph is timely and a forerunner of a spate of conceptual and empirical studies that we can expect in the near future.

Scheirer's monograph provides an agenda of what needs to be done. She reviews relevant literature, sets up a conceptual model—what is termed a social systems perspective—and examines its applicability to two mental health settings by both qualitative and quantitative research. Her work has limitations, of course. She might have gone farther afield in taking into account additional past conceptualizing and empirical implementation studies, her conceptual model could be more elaborate in some ways, and her field studies are primarily the work of a single investigation or limited to two mental health programs. Dr. Scheirer is aware of the limitations of her work and is appropriately modest in her claims of generality. Indeed, given the shortage of careful work and the press for ways to improve program implementation, she may be accused of being overly modest. The ideas and "principles" she provides in her last chapter, based upon her thoughtful consideration of the process of implementation and her research findings, have implications for—and should challenge—program sponsors, planners and providers in *all* human service fields. Moreover, her monograph will be useful in providing students in schools of health sciences and health services, social welfare, education, and urban planning with a concrete and orderly perspective on how to plan, design, and implement programs.

Finally, evaluation researchers will profit from her work; almost all evaluators have come to realize that there is little point and gratification in assessing programs with low probabilities of impact success because of faulty implementation. Scheirer's report provides a highly useful education for those of us who see our role to be much more than the application of technical procedures and seek to expand it to include influencing program implementation activities so as to maximize chances of successful outcomes. It may also encourage some of us to venture into the difficult research area of studying program implementation ourselves. Both Richard Berk and I believe readers will share our pleasure in having Mary Ann Scheirer's monograph in Sage's *Contemporary Evaluation Research* series.

—Howard E. Freeman
—Richard A Berk

1

Introduction

One fall, a small cricket found himself becoming colder and colder with each passing evening as the weather turned wintery. So he went to the wise old owl of the forest and said to him, "Oh wise old owl, please tell me what to do. The weather is getting colder and every evening I shiver and shake with the cold. If I don't do something soon, I know I will soon freeze to death. What can I do?"

"The answer to that is simple," said the wise old owl. "Just turn yourself into a grasshopper, and hibernate for the winter."

"But how can I turn myself into a grasshopper, oh wise old owl?" asked the cricket.

Replied the owl, "Humph, don't bother me with details. I've given you the principle. You implement it."

Over the past fifteen years, a torrent of social programs have been created to ameliorate problems in education, mental health, job training, and other areas. All too often a principle that is supposed to solve a problem has been enunciated by a "wise old owl."

The principle may be checked against the opinions of other experts in the field, examined for its political popularity, and sometimes even carefully field-tested. Official decisions translate the principle into a program and adopt it on a wide scale. Sometimes, data are collected to evaluate the outcomes of the program, but very little attention is paid to the "details" of implementing the program in the field. How innovative social programs are incorporated into the daily work routines of teachers, employment counselors, mental health workers, and others who are supposed to deliver the program tends to be relegated by default to the ingenuity and dedication of each local implementor.

Planning for new social programs has tended to emphasize the ideas or theories connecting a new social policy with desired outcomes, and/or the political maneuvers for getting the program adopted by relevant decision makers such as Congress, local school boards, or state mental health authorities. Little emphasis has been placed on detailed specification of the processes by which the policy or program would be translated into practice. As one analyst of implementation puts it, responsibility for implementation of federal programs tends to slip "between the cracks" of the system, with officials at each level assuming it is someone else's responsibility (Williams, 1976a). But this situation is beginning to be recognized as a "missing link" (Hargrove, 1975) in the complex chain of events that must occur if a theoretically valid new program is even to be tested within real situations. Not only must the theory behind the social innovation be valid, but it must be implemented in the day-to-day routine of the target social agency in order for the program to produce any measurable effects.

A number of analytical and empirical studies are now available which stimulate development of a systematic study of implementation. These were the basis for the first focus of this research project, which was to develop a social systems conceptual model of the variables likely to influence implementation processes. Rather than being considered entirely an administrative "art" drawing on personal expertise, implementation is treated here as a topic for social research, to search for regularities in implementation processes that will apply to several kinds of organizations. Such regularities, if documented, would contribute both to finding solutions to practical implementation problems and to extending knowledge of interpersonal behavior in organizational settings. This monograph is intended as a contribution to this developing body of implementation research, focusing particularly on the "micro-implementation" problem (Berman, 1978) of analyzing the change processes which occur within local organizations after a decision is made to adopt a new program.

The major thrust of this research report is an examination of the applicability of the conceptual model to case studies of the implementation of therapeutic innovations in two mental health centers. Field studies at the centers incorporated several data collection methods, including intensive interviews, extracting data from official records, document review, and nonparticipant observation. While it is, of course, impossible to test the generalizability of a conceptual model from two case studies, the purpose here was to explore the interrelationships of variables suggested by previous studies using intensive case study methods. By examining in some depth the processes that occurred in these situations, this study illustrates the utility of the model as a first step toward empirical explanation of implementation processes.

The purpose of the research reported here is thus to contribute to—and, it is hoped, to stimulate other additions to—the development of an empirically based study of implementation. The hypothesized relationships among the components of a social system undergoing the change necessary to implement a new program can and should be tested by rigorous field studies. Just as the theoretical principles underlying the substance of a new program should be validated by empirical assessments, so should the principles attempting to explain how programs are put into place be subject to verification. In this way, the implications of the term "implementation" can be specified for use in developing further research, advising policy makers, and helping program practitioners achieve higher levels of implementation.

No precise definition of "implementation" has been developed thus far, but most analysts use the term to refer to the process of carrying out a policy or program decision (Pressman and Wildavsky, 1973; Williams, 1976a). As recent analysts have emphasized, the decision to adopt a program does not automatically bring about the necessary actions to put the program into effect; there must be subsequent decisions on details, negotiations over responsibilities, assembly of resources and participants, and so forth. These are the processes that are covered by the general term "implementation." Since the processes are bound to be complex, a more precise definition is probably impossible without including within the definition some of the analyst's theoretical orientation toward the problem. For example, Berman and McLaughlin (1974: 13) define implementation as "the change process that occurs when an innovative project impinges upon an organization," which reflects their emphasis on implementation as a process of mutual adaptation between an organization and an educational innovation. For this reason, further definition of implementation depends on the specification of the researcher's theoretical approach.

A useful distinction is drawn by Berman's (1978) discussion of macro- and micro-implementation problems. Focusing on social policies adopted by the federal government, Berman notes that there is a set of problems associated with "macro-implementation," the ways in which government agencies specify and execute the policy in order to influence local delivery organizations in desired directions. Macro-implementation involves the translation of policies by successive layers of federal agency personnel to stimulate a compliance or adoption decision from local agencies. Micro-implementation processes refer to the changes necessary within the local organization to implement the decisions; Berman notes that the problems of delivery at this level involve the social system of local environmental influences and structural features, as well as individual differences among deliverers. The research reported here is addressed to problems of micro-implementation, in Berman's terms, with the development and application of an analytical model of organizational components which influence implementation within local organizations. No further analysis or discussion of macro-implementation problems is included.

The absence of precise definitions of "implementation" has meant that measurements of the extent of implementation have been constructed individually for each new study. Several major multiorganizational studies of the change processes surrounding implementation (Berman and McLaughlin, 1978; Beyer and Trice, 1978; Yin, 1979) have used tailor-made measures derived from interviews as dependent variables. Recent analyses of program evaluation methodology (Patton, 1979; Sechrest and Rednor, 1979; Rossi et al., 1979) have called for measurement of the "treatment" being evaluated as well as the outcomes, but most actual evaluations to date have not included specific measurement of the extent of program implementation.

Thus, measurement of implementation has not been cumulative, nor have generalized instruments been developed that provide rigorous assessment of implementation across various types of programs. One exception to this conclusion is the Levels of Use scale developed by Hall and his colleagues (Hall and Loucks, 1977; Loucks et al., 1975; Loucks and Melle, 1980) along with its extension by Leithwood and Montgomery (1980); but even this technique is based on the implementor's self-assessment obtained via an interview. Further, a few studies which have compared Levels of Use ratings with observational measures of implementation (Gersten and Carnine, 1980; Loucks and Melle, 1980) do not exhibit cross-method valida-. tion: the LoU scores tend to portray a higher extent of implementation, but less variability, than do behavioral observations. For the research reported here, measures of the extent of implementation by individual staff members were derived from existing institutional records and from interviews. These measures are described and compared in Chapter 3. However, the overall problem of the measurement of implementation remains; the complexity of the changes involved in implementation processes so far has defied efforts to capture them rigorously with single measurements.

The problem of social program implementation within local organizations can draw upon the extensive theory and research literature on social behavior and its change within organizations. If the innovative program involves delivery of a service by local "front-line" civil servants, as do many new developments in mental health, education, and employment training, then the role relationships between deliverer and recipient have to be designed or modified to accommodate the innovation. At this level, implementation becomes a problem of changing individual employee behavior to incorporate the new program, which in turn requires reciprocating modifications in the organizational structures which surround the individual employees. Thus, the extensive literature on both individual change and organizational change become potentially relevant to considering implementation problems within the innovating organization.

This body of literature was the basis for developing a model of implementation processes using a social system perspective. The model to be presented in Chapter 2 includes three levels of organizational analysis, each level with several components. Although the separation of such components in an analytical discussion at points may make them appear to be structural entities, the model is intended to be understood as composed of dynamic processes with mutually contingent interrelationships over time. Within this perspective, variability in program implementation is presented as resulting from the whole system of processes in the organization into which the program is introduced. No single component of the model is expected to account for the success or failure of implementation efforts.

In turn, the empirical study of implementation can contribute to underlying knowledge about behavior in organizations. Application of a social system perspective in the demanding context of real attempts to modify organizational outputs can help to test the usefulness of this theoretical perspective. Several competing perspectives, such as those emphasizing individual "resistance to change" or opening communication channels, can be examined for their ability to illuminate the behavior of employees charged with implementing a new program.

While such broad, competing perspectives are probably too diffuse to be directly tested by any single research study, even one much more extensive in scope than the research to be reported here, the weight of evidence across many such studies—particularly if future studies include intervention attempts to increase implementation—may contribute to greater confidence in the explanatory power of one perspective over another. In both laboratory experimentation and field research, the best test of one's understanding of a phenomenon is to be able to predict the outcomes of changes or manipulations in the system under study. In addition, the type of research reported here encourages combining in a single empirical analysis a number of concepts about organizational behavior that are often studied separately. Such a synthesis of organizational components helps develop and strengthen a systems perspective on life in organizations.

This report addresses some research gaps in the implementation literature by, first, developing an analytical model of organizational processes that are likely to influence the extent and manner of program implementation at the local level. Chapter 2 presents this model, after an overview of several perspectives on planned social change. The second focus is to apply the analytical model to field studies of two mental health organizations undertaking innovative programs. The more extensive study is an examination of a program at a developmental center which was intended to be adopted by all the treatment staff of the center. The scale of this program permitted sufficient data from institutional records and staff interviews to enable quantitative examination via regression analysis of propositions from the model developed in Chapter 2. Chapter 3 discusses the methodology for this field study at the developmental center, while Chapter 4 presents the results of both qualitative and quantitative analyses. The second field study involved a program being implemented on only one ward of a psychiatric center. The small scale of this program did not yield enough data for quantitative analysis but does permit a second qualitative assessment of the utility of the proposed analytical model, which is presented in Chapter 5. The sixth chapter compares findings from the two situations and presents overall conclusions. In summary, this monograph appraises the goodness of fit between a model of implementation processes and the behaviors of staff members undertaking new programs in two organizations.

2

Implementation and Organizational Change

A recent extensive survey studied the extent of local educational change resulting from four federally funded programs (Berman and Pauly, 1975; Berman and McLaughlin, 1978). After examining 293 projects in 18 states, the researchers found that although federal funds stimulated the initiation of many projects, few of these innovations were successfully implemented and fewer still were continued after federal funding ceased. After this intensive examination of local change processes, one of the researchers concluded that

> implementation, rather than educational treatment, level of resources or type of federal funding strategy, dominates the innovative process and its outcomes [McLaughlin, 1976:169].

Another study analyzed a project of the Economic Development Administration which aimed to increase minority employment in Oakland, California, by a massive subsidy of public works (Pressman and Wildavsky, 1973). Although $23 million was allocated to this project in 1966, only $3 million was actually spend by 1969 and only a handful of new jobs were created. The authors analyzed why implementation of this project was so difficult when political conflict was minimal, finances were available, and overall agreements were made early. They concluded that many of the difficulties resulted from the

> inability of the machinery for implementation to move fast enough to capture the agreements while they lasted. . . . The apparently simple and straightforward is really complex and convoluted. . . . What seemed to be a simple program turned out to be a very complex one, involving numerous participants, a host of differing perspectives, and a long and tortuous path of decision points that had to be cleared [Pressman and Wildavsky, 1973: 92-94]

A third study reported the results of a large-scale field experiment testing methods of introducing an innovative treatment into mental health organizations (Fairweather et al., 1974). Although clear evidence was available showing effective outcomes from the program, few hospitals were willing to adopt it. Of 255 mental hospitals contacted in the experiment, only five were continuing to expand use of the new program after two years. The authors conclude:

> It seems obvious that a mechanism for creating continuous change in mental health organizations is necessary if new programs are to be incorporated into existing health practices. . . . Historically, much of the effort in the mental health area has been devoted to creating new treatment programs, yet little attention has been paid to the adoption of beneficial programs by mental health organizations [Fairweather et al., 1974: 181] .

These examples of the growing importance placed on implementation processes by a number of policy analysts demonstrate the impetus for the present study. Within the past ten years, federal, state and local agencies have greatly expanded their use of social research, particularly in attempts to evaluate the outcomes of a multitude of social programs. Yet the results of these evaluations, especially when they are well designed methodologically, frequently can document no outcome effects attributable to the program (Gilbert et al., 1975; Gordon and Morse, 1975). One prime reason for the lack of positive effects may be that the programs were poorly implemented. As the above quotations illustrate, implementation is a complex but understudied problem that can easily undermine well-conceived social programs. Whatever the theory behind an innovation, the change must be implemented in the day-to-day routine of the target social agency in order for it to produce measurable effects.

Implementation research can be viewed as an application of social scientists' research concepts to the problems of applied social change. Although a large body of social science literature exists attempting to analyze and explain, synthesize and predict the mechanisms of social change, this research has not focused on the specific processes surrounding implementation. As this chapter will detail, a growing body of analytical and empirical studies are now available from which one can develop a systematic framework for the examination of implementation processes.

With an integrated framework, many of the previously scattered themes on influences on implementation can be combined to provide a more systematic perspective for future empirical investigations. The framework developed here can also provide an overview of factors to be examined by program managers facing implementation problems. The purpose of this chapter, therefore, is to integrate findings from past studies of implementation into a social systems framework, thus specifying organizational processes that are likely to influence the extent and manner of program implementation at the local level.

THEORETICAL PERSPECTIVES ON PLANNED SOCIAL CHANGE

Efforts toward the scientific study of social change have evolved from many different disciplines, each pursuing favorite variables. Consequently, fragmented results from various studies have not built up a coherent body of tested propositions that can readily be applied to planners' concrete problems. While there are at present relatively few empirical studies specifically addressing implementation as a topic for research, the literature devoted to social change in general is enormous, with numerous propositions and findings that might relate to understanding implementation. Each social science discipline seems to have one or more strands of theory addressing problems of social change, but so far no synthesis has emerged which weaves together these diverse threads of discourse.

While a full consideration of previous approaches to organizational change falls beyond the scope of this review, this chapter will begin by outlining six perspectives for studying change within organizations to examine their potential contribution to a study of implementation. Current literature on planned change reveals five perspectives suggesting how much change does take place, plus one perspective focusing on why many attempted programs fail to be sustained. While these six perspectives are not always mutually exclusive in particular analysts' discussions of change processes, they will be treated separately here to enhance clarity. This discussion has benefited from Elmore's (1978) paper presenting four organizational models for implementation, but does not follow his treatment exactly.

RATIONAL PLANNING

Perhaps the most prominent tradition in the analysis of planned social change could be labeled the "rationalist school." Generally writing from a normative-advisory stance, proponents of this school emphasize rational planning via problem definition, assessment of alternative solutions, choice of "best" solution with cost-benefit calculations, and implementation of the chosen program by information-transfer training for staff at operational levels (Havelock et al., 1970; Kunkel, 1975). The focus of most empirical analyses is on processes surrounding the decision to adopt a new program or policy, with much less emphasis on the implementation phase. If less than full implementation is discussed at all by proponents of this perspective, it is likely to be treated as resulting from a failure to adequately analyze the problem, thus resulting in an inappropriate solution, or from allowing "political" considerations to override rational decision-making. The essence of this perspective is that planned change should utilize rational planning concerning the expected outcomes of various alternatives in the process of reaching a decision. If implementation processes are problematic, then assessment of implementation strengths and weaknesses should be included in the planning.

STRUCTURAL ANALYSIS

A second perspective might be labeled the "structural study of innovativeness in organizations." These researchers disavow attempts to prescribe what managers *should* do, focusing instead on empirical assessments of characteristics that distinguish innovating from noninnovating organizations (for example, Baldridge and Burnham, 1975; Hage and Aiken, 1967). Deriving particularly from sociological research on structural determinants of organizational behavior, such studies have found that propensity to innovate is positively influenced by a production task subject to rapidly changing technologies and/or markets, such as in electronic firms (Burns and Stalker, 1961); by decentralization in decision-making processes (Hage and Aiken, 1967); by greater size and complexity of organization, in the case of school districts (Baldridge and Burham, 1975); and by strong communication links with outside sources of innovative ideas (Corwin, 1972). While researchers using this perspective have extended valuable empirical analysis to this topic, the focus has been mostly on the decision-to-adopt phase of planned change, with little analysis of whether the decisions were actually implemented by the organization in question. Since "innovativeness" is usually operationally defined as the number of new programs or technologies accepted in a given period of time, with data collected by surveys of organizational informants, this perspective is just beginning to contribute empirical data on what happens to innovations after the decision processes are completed (see Beyer and Trice, 1978).

ORGANIZATIONAL DEVELOPMENT

A third perspective on organizational change, which incorporates elements of several others, is the applied management
strategy termed "organizational development" (Beckhard,
1969; Schmuck and Miles, 1971). As an intervention strategy,
consultants using this approach emphasize change *of* the organizational system, such as by decentralization of decision-
making or opening up communication patterns, rather than
change *within* a system necessary to implement a specific innovation. A management intervention program using this strategy
might include T-groups or other group exercises, data feedback
from perceptions of organizational processes, and so on. Underlying this approach is the assumption that increasing general
openness to innovation within an organization is a necessary
requirement for change to occur at all; the implication is that
attempts to introduce an innovative program in a centralized,
hierarchical bureaucracy without first changing its structure
would inevitably fail.

A rigorous empirical investigation of the use of organizational
development techniques was incorporated into Tornatzky and
his colleagues' experiments (Tornatzky et al., 1980) promoting
the implementation of community lodge programs by mental
hospitals. Within an experimental design, the use of organizational development techniques and the extent of staff participation were, in fact, manipulated by the researchers. The results
showed some effectiveness for these techniques on the extent of
implementation but also documented the presence of preexisting organizational characteristics which dominated the outcomes of the implementation attempts.

The proposition that participation in decision-making will
induce individual staff members to accept the decisions reached,
which derives from the Coch and French (1948) experiments on
group decision-making, has led to an extensive movement advocating "participatory management." An example of the use
of this perspective is found in Fullan's (1972) review of studies
on educational change, which examines empirical examples of
attempted educational change, mostly failures of implementation, and then concludes that only radical restructuring of

schools toward group process decisions by the users (teachers, students, parents) can enable program innovations to be successful. More recently, Berman's advocacy of "adaptive implementation" (1980a) incorporates some of the same focus on participation by the users. Thus, the organizational development perspective is not a distinct theoretical approach, since advocates explicitly apply concepts derived from the other approaches outlined here. Instead, organizational development is a normative "bottom-up" counter to the rationalist "top-down" strategy.

DIFFUSION OF INNOVATIONS

Two further perspectives on change in organizations focus more strongly on the role of individuals. The fourth perspective, labeled the "diffusion of innovations," derives from studies of the introduction of new technologies into rural communities and non-Western nations. Although this approach was developed initially by anthropologists and rural sociologists, Rogers and Shoemaker's review (1971) of more than a thousand empirical studies points out that diffusion research is now being done in fields such as education, marketing, medical sociology, and communication. The common theme of these studies is to examine elements in a communication system surrounding the adoption by individuals of new ideas or technologies. Particular emphasis is placed on studying the characteristics of adopters, of communication channels, and of the innovations themselves, as well as examination of the roles of change agents and opinion leaders.

When this approach is applied to organizations undertaking new programs, (see Baldridge and Burnham, 1975; Corwin, 1972; Rogers and Shoemaker, 1971: chap. 10), the focus for study has usually been on the *decision* to adopt a new program, rather than on processes influencing implementation. For this reason, until recently, the extensive body of empirical research done within this tradition did not directly illuminate problems of implementation. More recently, some diffusion analysts have broadened their conceptualizations to include change processes subsequent to the decision to adopt (for example, Radnor et al.,

1978). Several hypotheses developed by the diffusion research-ers will be included in the framework for the examination of implementation to be specified below.

INDIVIDUAL PSYCHOLOGY

A fifth set of theories sometimes applied to planned change in organizations arises from the large psychological literature on individual change. The extensive studies on attitudes, attitude change, and the relationship between attitudes and behavior (reviewed by Fishbein and Ajzen, 1975; Keisler et al., 1969; Schuman and Johnson, 1976) promote the view that individual beliefs, evaluations, and other cognitions about a change pro-gram influence that individual's willingness to carry out the program; yet the direction of influence between changes in attitudes and changes in behavior has remained controversial (Bem, 1972; Schuman and Johnson, 1976). A related empirical research tradition is the study of individual change in attitudes via persuasive communications (Hoveland et al., 1953), which is somewhat similar to the diffusion literature in examining the characteristics of the communicator, the communication itself, and the recipient to determine how individual attitude change may be induced.

These basic psychological studies have been applied to change in organizations by management consultants and others as propositions for overcoming individual "resistance to change" (see Watson, 1973). For example, the "unfreezing-moving-re-freezing" change sequence proposed by Lewin (1947) has been used as a model for developing acceptance of technological interventions (Zand and Sorensen, 1975). But a review by Gross, Giacquinta, and Bernstein (1971) of the literature on overcoming individual resistance to change points out that this research has largely ignored the organizational context for change and that actual evidence is sparse on the degree to which individual resistance impedes change when the organizational environment supports it. However, the underlying assumption of all the individual change approaches, that implementing staff members' cognitions—attitudes, beliefs, feelings of participa-tion, and so forth—are important factors in organization change processes, is a perspective that is highly relevant to an overview of implementation.

BUREAUCRATIC AND POLITICAL MODELS

A sixth perspective on problems of organizational change might be more accurately termed the "bureaucratic-political explanations for nonimplementation." Developed as a reaction to the rationalist planned change model described above, the bureaucratic and political perspectives are well illustrated by Allison's (1971) examination of decision-making surrounding the 1962 Cuban missile crisis and by Warwick's analysis (1975) of attempted reorganization in the U.S. State Department. In Allison's analysis, the rationalist view is contrasted to a bureaucratic model in which participating agencies act in terms of their standard operating procedures, and to a political model in which interacting individuals pursue both their own and their agencies' interests.

This perspective has been developed by a number of policy analysts who focus on federal policy. For example, Pincus (1974) uses this perspective for an analysis of incentives for innovation in public schools. He points out that school administrators' adoption of innovations may stem from several incentives having little to do with changing pupil outcomes, such as satisfying various publics which make demands on the schools, attracting additional resources from external funding agencies, and/or projecting the image of progressive administration for attracting peer approval or career advancement. Similarly, Pressman and Wildavsky's (1973) analysis of the Economic Development Administration's Oakland project and Walter Williams' several analyses of implementation problems (1976b, 1980) focus on the bureaucratic layers and political interests that intervene between the decision to undertake a program and its eventual action component in the field. Another offshoot of this perspective has been to emphasize the extent to which the clarity of a federal policy or statute, and the structure of management processes specified by legislation, can have profound influence even on local implementation processes (Sabatier and Mazmanian, 1980; Bullock, 1980).

In summary, these six theoretical perspectives found in literature about induced organizational change provide quite different orientations toward constructing a conceptual model for the examination of implementation. Should one emphasize rational planning oriented toward program goals or stress understanding the bureaucratic-political forces dominating day-to-day organizational life? Is change best accomplished by attention to employee beliefs, attitudes, or other sources of "resistance to change" or by a focus on organizational structural properties such as centralization and complexity? Does the apparent convergence from several perspectives on user participation in decision-making (also termed decentralization, or, in the diffusion literature, as meeting users' felt needs) mean that programs designed by professionals are doomed to failure? Is obtaining support from the top of an organizational hierarchy, a "top-down" strategy, more vital for success than the commitment of lower-level employees actually implementing the program, a "bottom-up" strategy? That few answers are presently available for these questions of approach to implementation will be apparent by the lack of strong evidence for or against many hypotheses about implementation. However, to anticipate the conclusions of this literature review and model development, it is likely that both sides of all of the above questions will show useful implications for analysis of an applied problem such as program implementation.

AN ANALYTICAL FRAMEWORK FOR
THE STUDY OF PROGRAM IMPLEMENTATION

This review of approaches and limitations in six theoretical perspectives on planned change in organizations has revealed a lack of analytical consensus regarding the most meaningful approach to the problems of program implementation. Like the six blind men examining an elephant, each theoretical school emphasizes different aspects of the change process, but thus far no synthesizing model has been developed to integrate findings from diverse approaches.

Nevertheless, such a synthesis of previous studies is possible by viewing the implementing organization as a social system.

This perspective, which is derived from the open system organizational model developed by Katz and Kahn (1966) emphasizes the processes and interrelationships among three levels of analysis for examining organizational phenomena. The first is the macro level of the organization as a whole, including interchange between the organization and its environment. The second is the intermediate level of organizational subunits and the processes which regulate their daily work activities. The third is the micro level of individual members' behaviors, motivations, and cognitions. An outline of the framework is presented in Table 2.1.

This integrated social system perspective for analyzing implementation is thus a seventh theoretical approach to the study of implementation, although it builds upon and explicitly incorporates many variables suggested by the six approaches just reviewed. As the following detailed discussion will show, variables occurring at each of the organizational levels may substantively influence the implementation process; an attempt to focus on one or the other of the whole set of components as *the* keys to successful implementation is likely to promote neglect of other concurrent processes that are equally vital.

For clarity, I will first discuss the component processes at each level of the framework as they individually influence implementation. Some hypotheses relating each component to implementation in general will be specified in order to suggest potentially testable propositions at each level. While additional hypotheses undoubtedly could be generated, these examples are presented to emphasize the potential for empirical research at all levels of the conceptual model. Further, hypotheses derived from studies focusing on one aspect of the framework may contradict other hypotheses about other components. This set of hypotheses is thus not intended as an integrated theoretical model, but instead reveals the range of possible influences on the complex processes of implementation. The sometimes contradictory implications of hypotheses generated by past research emphasize as well the need for future research of sufficiently wide scope to compare influences from several levels.

Although the separation of the components in an analytical discussion may at points make them appear to be structural

TABLE 2.1
Outline of the Analytical Framework
for the Study of Social Program Implementation

Macro-Level Components

    Decision processes
    Control processes
    Obtaining resources
    Relations with the environment

Intermediate-Level Processes

    Supervisory expectations
    Standard operating routines
    Technical requirements of the innovation
    Communication flow
    Work group norms

Individual-Level Variables

    Behavioral skills
    Incentives
    Cognitive supports

entities, the model is intended to be understood as composed of dynamic processes with mutually contingent interrelationships over time. Within this perspective, variability in program implementation is presented as resulting from the whole system of processes in the organization into which the program is introduced. No single component of the model is expected to account for the success or failure of implementation efforts.

After the component processes at each level are analyzed, some interrelationships among the organization levels will be suggested, along with a more dynamic process model of implementation over time. However, research on such interrelationships has been too sparse to yield many detailed hypotheses specifying these dynamic relationships.

MACRO-LEVEL COMPONENTS

Although organizations are constructed from the actions of individual human beings, the organization as a whole can also be considered an entity or unit of analysis. On this analytical level, decisions are reached by legitimated organizational authorities which direct employees toward specific actions (although such decisions are not always carried out); the organization acquires and uses resources such as staff time and financial support; and pressures from both organizations and individuals in its environment are received and processed. It is organizational processes at this level of analysis that are here termed the macro-level components influencing implementation.

DECISION PROCESSES

Despite the rational perspective's exhortation that decision-making should proceed from a consideration of well-analyzed alternatives for reaching agreed-upon organizational goals, most studies of actual social program decision-making (for example, Williams and Elmore, 1976; Emrick and Peterson, 1978; Bardach, 1977; Pressman and Wildavksy, 1973), as well as several prominent organizational theorists (Allison, 1971; Cohen and March, 1974), have emphasized instead the political bargaining nature of many organizational decisions.

For example, Elmore (1975) states that the federal Follow Through educational program, ostensibly begun to test experimentally the efficacy of several educational models for disadvantaged children, was actually conceived as a political "holding action" by the Office of Economic Opportunity to keep some federal attention on primary school education until Congress approved a larger budget for massive elementary school aid. At the local level of Follow Through, Elmore notes, school districts were selected for participation on the basis of political—not educational or experimental—factors. While each district formally chose the educational model to be tried there, this did not mean that local decision makers understood the implications of the model chosen, nor that individual teachers had participated in the decision, according to the developer and sponsor of one of the participating models (Weikart and Banet, 1975). This political decision-making surrounding the initiation of Follow Through is not an isolated occurrence. Evidence on this point is provided by a number of additional studies: Campeau and her colleagues' evaluation (1979) of Project Information Packaging as an educational dissemination technique; Emrick and Peterson's (1978) review of findings from five studies of educational dissemination and change; Herriott and Gross's (1979) case studies of attempts to introduce comprehensive change into rural school districts; and Farrar, DeSanctis, and Cohen's (1979) paper illustrating the multitude of local perspectives which influenced Experience Based Career Education.

Thus, a useful starting point for implementation analysis is to examine the interests involved in the decision to adopt the program, particularly using the bureaucratic and political perspective. Whose program it is and what are their stakes? Were those who were most influential in the adoption of a program most interested in the fact of program adoption (for example, to secure additional financial resources or personal career advancement) or in achieving the outcomes the program was intended to produce? A Rand Corporation survey of 293 educational change projects (Berman and McLaughlin, 1974) analyzed this distinction as an opportunity-based versus a problem-solving decision to adopt; they found stronger likelihood of implementation for a new program undertaken to address a perceived problem. A similar conclusion emerged from an experimentally designed examination of attempts to introduce a "lodge" program into 255 mental hospitals (Fairweather et al., 1974).

Subsequent to the inital decision to adopt an innovative program, supplementary negotiations over the details of implementation may require further decision-making. Bardach's analysis of implementation "games" (1977) emphasizes that the parties to such negotiations often have numerous interests in addition to promoting the formal program goals: Players may be obtaining "easy money" for their particular sphere of influence, deflecting program goals toward key constituencies in "piling on," or making sure that potential future difficulties are "not our problem." The interests represented in negotiations about program details thus influence heavily the strategies adopted for translating the overall program into operational reality.

Further, those influencing a new program decision may or may not be in a position to enforce the decision. Federal program administrators are often in a low enforcement capability position vis-à-vis local officials, as has been found by analysts of federal educational initiatives (Pincus, 1974), employment stimulation activities (Pressman and Wildavsky, 1973), and urban redevelopment (Banfield, 1976; Derthick, 1976). Even within a particular organization, if those most favorable toward a proposed new innovation are not in direct "line" positions of supervision over implementing staff members, implementation is likely to be more difficult than if those with supervisory control are strong supporters of a new program.

Several hypotheses about decision-making can thus be derived from previous studies. Implementation is likely to be facilitated if those most influential in the decision to adopt the program are oriented toward problem-solving rather than toward personal or organizational opportunity. Second, implementation will be facilitated if those influential in program decisions, both initial and subsequent, are in a high enforcement position (that is, a "line" administrative relationship) over those implementing the program.

CONTROL PROCESSES

One of the most widely held, but still controversial, propositions in organizational theory is the participation hypothesis: that those influenced by a particular decision should participate in its formulation in order to create commitment to and thus implementation of the decision. This is a central theme of the organizational development perspective, but it is also included in structural analysis. Within the structural perspective, this is similar to the evidence that decentralization of decision-making promotes innovativeness in general (Hage and Aiken, 1967; Corwin, 1972), as well as facilitating the implementation of specific policies (Beyer and Trice, 1977; Fairweather et al., 1974; Holland, 1973). Recent evidence is provided by a major experimental intervention study by Tornatzky et al. (1980) in which the inclusion of staff from various organizational levels was found to facilitate adoption and implementation of the intervention studied—the lodge program in mental hospitals— but the participation of a larger number of staff, per se, did not lead to these outcomes.

Several competing theoretical explanations could account for a link between participation and implementation (see Lawler, 1976). Actual political power to secure decisions consistent with their own interests should yield satisfaction and commitment from lower-level employees, and implementing the decision would then further their own interests. Following a second theoretical linkage, the value of participation may be great even if it does not include actual decision-making power, if such participation provides accurate informational feedback to higher administrators who then control decision outcomes toward directions acceptable to other staff members. A third type of explanation for the benefits of participation focuses on the work group consensus generated in the process of group participation; by this explanation, individual employees would strive to carry out the decision if they believed it to be the behavior approved by a relevant peer group. Thus, the implications of centralized or decentralized control processes for the implementation of a specific program are not yet clear, since the causal mechanism for any effect of participation is still ambiguous.

A further complication is that several analysts point to strong interest and support from central administrators as necessary for furthering implementation (McLaughlin, 1976; Greenblatt et al., 1971), while at the same time advocating the involvement of the ultimate users of the innovation. If an organization's usual control processes are centralized, then most initiatives for changes in policies and routines come "down through channels." In this case, the introduction of a new program from outside the usual channels without the strong support of central administrators is likely to be ignored by those who are accustomed to receiving job rewards or reprimands from their supervisors. Implementing a new program not supported by one's superiors might be suicidal for continued employment in such a situation.

Perhaps the only way to reconcile these apparently conflicting viewpoints concerning control processes is to hypothesize that the strategy for introducing a specific innovation should be congruent with the organization's prevalent control process, whether participatory or centralized. Further, it is likely that implementation will be facilitated if those directly responsible for day-to-day implementation participate in the decision regarding adoption, although the mechanism underlying such participation needs further clarification. Finally, it is hypothesized that implementation will be higher if central administrators strongly and actively support the program.

OBTAINING RESOURCES

A third macro-level component which vitally affects the course of implementation involves obtaining adequate resources of personnel, time, and financial support for the program. This component has been most often emphasized by analysts using the political-bureaucratic perspective, although planning for resource utilization is also, of course, part of the rational planning approach.

While it seems obvious that a program requiring new materials or new staff members necessitates some level of additional financial support from the organization, just what is the minimum level beyond which the program will certainly fail is probably impossible to specify a priori. Several educational case studies have noted that a major factor in teachers' inability to put more individualized, pupil-centered educational innovations into practice was the lack of promised curricular materials that would provide self-motivated instruction for the students (Gross et al., 1971; Smith and Keith, 1971). This lack of key materials was probably due to inadequate overall financial support only in the Gross study, while in Smith and Keith's analysis major problems related to delays in completion of the open-space building as well as late arrival of classroom materials. However, the important point may be that teachers *perceived* a necessity for new materials; without them, the teachers were reluctant to attempt role changes in their interaction with pupils.

Overall level of funding was one of the variables studied in the Rand survey of 293 educational change projects. It was *not* found to be a significant predictor of any measure of implementation (Berman and Pauly, 1975). Fairweather's experiment on innovation in mental hospitals (1974) did not find level of hospital resources to be a major factor in adopting change. Further, Yin's (1979) analysis of the "routinization" of hardware innovations by public bureaucracies refutes the ideas that the level of funding, or the transfer from federal to local funding, are key factors leading to the long-term incorporation of change, for neither of these resource factors were related to the continued use of a variety of innovations.

Similar findings regarding staff numbers emerged from an analysis of attempted individualization of therapy in the 28 wards of a large mental hospital. The differences in staff/patient ratios among the wards did not account for the fairly large differences in patient management practices found after a three-year program (Holland, 1973). Instead, organizational structural variables, such as decentralization within the wards and the participation of lower-level staff in planning meetings, were key determinants of the outcomes

Another resource often overlooked in the planning for new programs is time, considered in terms of both daily schedules and adequate time for the intervention to show effects. Case studies of programs requiring changes in staff behavior illustrate that staff meetings, planning new materials, working out role relationships, and solving interpersonal conflicts inevitably take substantial amounts of staff time, which, if it must be added to normal job requirements, leads to role overload or staff exhaustion (see Smith and Keith, 1971; Weatherley and Lipsky, 1977). The time resources required can be a major problem in the organizational development perspective on change discussed above, for reaching group consensus on objectives and procedures often requires extensive staff meetings and therefore time lost from other duties.

Further, decision makers frequently allow too few months for a program to be implemented before requiring evaluations of outcome effects. For example, the Office of Economic Opportunity launched a large-scale "experiment" with educational performance contracting in just six months. Those six months' efforts include the initial decision; contracting with private companies whose level of payment was to depend on student performance; selection of school districts, schools, and teachers; and negotiating relationships with teachers who were generally hostile to the whole concept (Gramlich and Koshel, 1975). Within one academic year, the performance contractors were required to implement their incentive-based programs and achieve student test scores that represented more than twice the normally expected rate of achievement in order for the company to make any profit. When the first year's test scores lagged substantially behind this level of accomplishment, the experiment was terminated as showing performance contracting to be a failure. A more adequate assessment would be that not nearly enough time was available for responsible planning and adequate implementation before evaluation of student achievement. The long time required for adequate implementation was also emphasized by Emrick and Peterson's (1978) examination of outside intervention as a means toward educational change, as well as by an intensive classroom observational study of the implementation of a highly structured teaching technology (Gersten and Carnine, 1980).

A sobering analysis of the delay time involved for multiple clearances of operating details is Pressman and Wildavsky's (1973) examination of a new construction project. When as many as 70 separate clearances were required for the project, each of which was favorable (although many were obtained from officials not highly committed to that project), the necessary negotiation time added nearly four years to the time required for translating the initial project agreement into beginning actual construction. "Haste makes waste" is certainly an aphorism that applies to program implementation.

For many new programs, simply obtaining financial backing is an undertaking that may require much staff effort and time *before* the program can begin. In one case study of the establishment of a neighborhood health center in a black ghetto (Milio, 1971), nearly four years of negotiations with existing community agencies failed to secure stable support, but new sources of federal funding obtained through new, powerful black community intermediaries finally allowed the center to open. The recurring problem with outside sources of funding, however, is that commitments made to secure it involve some loss of autonomy for the staff (Hage and Aiken, 1970) and may involve cooptation of significant degrees of control. Implementation may then be a serious problem if the outside agency with financial control has interests different from those the implementation of the program is likely to serve, such as satisfying political constituencies or creating a liberal image while preventing any real redistribution of social power.

To summarize this section, one can hypothesize that having adequate financial and staff resources to carry out a new program is a necessary component for implementation, but increasing staff or funding alone is not sufficient to stimulate effective motivation and coordination for change. Further, planning for implementation should include adequate time both for daily problem-solving activities and for longer-term processes to produce effects before requiring outcome evaluation. Finally, it is likely that the more frequently resources are obtained outside the organization's usual sources of support, the more difficult will be long-term implementation, because significant control may be coopted by the outside agency and because institutionalization of the program is prevented when no "local" resources are available. Thus, the problems encountered when obtaining program resources lead directly to another set of variables to be considered at the macro-level: environmental pressures.

RELATIONS WITH THE ENVIRONMENT

In this context, "the environment" refers not only to the physical environment but, more important, to the social environment of other organizations, political pressures, public opinion, and legal regulations which form the operationg context of every organization. Dimensions for characterizing environments have been described in diverse ways by several analysts (Hall, 1972; Stinchcombe, 1965; Thompson, 1967). A useful categorization for analyzing implementation is to adapt Thompson's discussion of four sectors of an industrial firm's task environment: customers, suppliers, competitors, and regulators. In the context of a human service organization these categories might be named beneficiaries, supporters (both financial and political), competing services, and regulators.

Beneficiaries' availability to participate in a new program is an obvious necessity for implementation and may be problematic if the clients are hard to contact or unwilling to participate, for example, in a drug abuse prevention program (see Chase, 1979). The political pressures from beneficiaries or their representatives (parents, community groups, and the like) can undermine implementation either by being opposed to a new concept or by outspoken support. Parental opposition to the innovations attempted was found to be a significant source of implementation difficulties by teachers in the Rand study (Berman and Pauly, 1975), as well as a problem for administrators and teachers in Smith and Keith's case study (1971). That outspoken support can also lead to problems is noted by a sponsor of one of the Follow Through model educational programs, who found that parental preoccupation with securing survival of the program in their own community hampered teachers' efforts to implement and evaluate an experimental educational curriculum (Weikart and Banet, 1975).

Danger of cooptation from financial supporters has already been discussed. In addition, a coalition of supporters assembled to secure adoption of a new policy or program may in fact pursue diverse goals during the process of implementation (see Bardach, 1977). In more detailed negotiations, then, supporters may undermine pursuit of outcome objectives, or the compromises needed to preserve the coalition may threaten the program staff's ability to pursue *any* objectives effectively.

While social service providers are not ordinarily thought to have competitors, in fact, a new program or service offered by one agency may be implicit criticism that another agency is failing to provide an adequate program for those clients. For example, an attempt to begin a behaviorally oriented mental health program for children was vigorously opposed by existing mental health agencies with traditional psychoanalytic orientations (Sarasen, 1972). Agencies are often in competition for funding from federal sources or community United Funds. They may also compete in recruiting or placing clients, in obtaining volunteer workers, or in securing affiliation with prestigious universities.

Finally, most human service agencies operate under numerous laws, regulations, and guidelines from state and federal agencies. Even if such regulations do not directly address or proscribe the changes attempted by a new program, the staff time occupied and bureaucratic compliance-with-directives orientation created by such regulations may inhibit staff initiative in solving implementation problems. Further, compliance with one set of regulations may directly counter the intent of a new program. For example, a school desegregation plan may scatter the intended target population for a specialized innovative program, such as a school curriculum emphasizing black culture. Regulations that are intended to secure the rights of beneficiaries, such as civil rights for mental health patients, may elicit primarily on-paper compliance from "street-level bureaucrats" who have too great a work load to encourage individual variability (see Weatherley and Lispky, 1977).

To analyze problems of relationships with the environment, it is necessary to reemphasize that the boundaries of a particular "system," and thus the designation of its environment or supersystem, depends to a large extent on the viewpoint of the investigator (Katz and Kahn, 1966). Thus, a local mental health agency can be viewed as an organization by itself, or as part of a state Department of Mental Hygiene, which is also constrained by federal regulations and funding mechanisms, or as part of a community's mental health "system," or as one small part of a nationwide cultural context of professional training, prestige, and power which regulates job roles for psychiatrists, psychologists, and social workers. What may be viewed as a "program" in one agency, such as the federal Office of Education, may be seen as a source of funding by local school districts. Responsibilities for policy and operations are often divided among several layers of agencies. In the resulting diffusion of responsibility for implementation, the original program goals often are lost, reinterpreted, or ignored (Williams, 1976b, 1980; Chase, 1979; Sabatier and Mazmanian, 1980; Levine, 1972). The overall relationships between organizations and their environments can have great impact on the implementation of specific programs, but attempting to untangle the strands of influence from federal policy initiatives is beyond the scope of this chapter.

It seems somewhat premature to specify hypotheses concerning the impact of environmental relationships on implementation processes. Certainly, any analysis of potential implementation problems should include the possibility of either support or opposition from beneficiaries, prior supporters, competing services, or regulators. It may be that the more diverse the external coalition supporting the initiation of a social program, the easier the political process leading to adoption of a program, but the more difficult actual program implementation becomes as elements of the supporting coalition pull in different directions. Concerning regulations, one can hypothesize that the larger the body of regulations affecting a particular organization, the more difficult is implementation of an innovative program, as staff become more compliance-oriented and as directly conflicting regulations become more likely. However, it may not be the sheer quantity of regulations that influences implementation, but rather the number of relatively recently passed rulings that are incompletely assimilated into organizational routines. In this case, another new program would strain organizational capacities for change in general.

The preceding four sets of organizational components—decision-making, control processes, obtaining resources, and relations with environments—all involve the macro level, or the organization considered as a whole. These macro-level processes form the context for the internal structures and procedures by which the day-to-day work is carried out; the macro level sets limits within which intermediate and individual factors operate. The theoretical perspectives which have contributed most heavily to investigation of this level of organizations are the political-bureaucratic perspective, rational planning, and structural analysis, all of which have traditionally focused on the total organization as the unit of analysis. What has been missing from analyses conducted from these perspectives is sufficient attention to the internal components of organizations, which also influence implementation.

INTERMEDIATE-LEVEL PROCESSES

Turning to the internal processes of the organization, a number of factors can be identified at the intermediate level which are likely to influence the implementation of a new program. By intermediate level is meant consideration of the subdivisions of the organization, which may differ within the same organization in type of work or of clients. Subdivisions usually have a distinct supervisory structure and are the work locations for individual staff members. Examples are wards within a hospital, schools within a school district, or academic departments within a university.

SUPERVISORY EXPECTATIONS

The tone and context for work within a subdivision is set by the role expectations of its supervisor(s) for the subordinates within that division. While accounts of the difficulties of implementation have frequently cited the importance of daily involvement of supervisors (Gersten and Carnine, 1980; Gross et al., 1971; Gramlich and Koshel, 1975; Herriott and Gross, 1979; Smith and Keith, 1971; Wilkinson, 1973), little emphasis has heretofore been placed on training or reorienting supervisors or on hiring new supervisors whose backgrounds and training are congruent with the theoretical orientation of a new program. Thus, a principal who has not taught using individualized instruction is not likely to be able to guide a teacher attempting to implement an open education program. The obvious dilemma is the fact that a program *is* innovative means that supervisors are not likely to have used the procedures when they were working at lower levels of the organization. Thus, supervisors need retraining and, frequently, reorientation of cognitive beliefs about appropriate methods of working with the organization's clients. Yet, if expertise in the program is available only from outside professional consultants, or from "staff" departments within the organization, the supervisor's own professional expertise is threatened; he or she is likely to resent being told "how to do my job" by an "outsider." Further, many supervisors enter their positions directly from a professional training program, rather than moving up from lower level positions. For example, nurses often supervise mental health ward aides, and college-trained administrators supervise clerical staff. In these cases as well, innovation in the lower-level employees' duties is likely to require reorientation of the supervisor's expectations.

Surprisingly little literature is available on the reciprocity of expectations between supervisors and their subordinates. In spite of the widely cited study of role conflict and role ambiguity by Kahn and his colleagues (Kahn et al., 1964), in which these personal stress indicators were found to be related to organizational positions such as boundary roles and middle management, relatively few studies have followed this lead by studying both supervisors' and subordinates' job perceptions. A study by Dornbush (1976) indicated that fewer than half of a sample of teachers could name the criteria on which they were evaluated by principals.

Several studies by Graen and his colleagues on role-making processes (Graen, 1976; Haga et al., 1974) suggest that many organizational roles and accompanying supervisory expectations are not well defined, bureaucratic slots with which employees must simply conform. Instead, even lower-level employees often have considerable latitude in the enactment of their jobs. In these circumstances, the introduction of a new program requiring changes in staff behavior necessitates a renegotiation of roles; whatever previous balance had been reached on operating routines or enforcement of rules may be incompatible with the procedures needed to implement the innovation.

Major changes in the behaviors or techniques required of implementors may also require new supervisory roles. For example, the recommended implementation process for the Direct Instruction Model of compensatory elementary education incorporates expert "resource teachers" who supervise other teachers rather than teaching classes of their own. The role of "resource teacher" includes observing other teachers trying to learn the Direct Instruction techniques, providing feedback on the appropriateness of their attempts, and modeling the new behaviors both in the classroom and during in-service training sessions (Gersten and Carnine, 1980). In this case, the school principals continue their former administrative roles, while the resource teachers provide technical consultation and supervision.

In short, supervisory expectations for both their own and their subordinates' roles may require examination and alteration for an innovation to be implemented. One can hypothesize that implementation will be facilitated if supervisors' backgrounds, in terms of disciplinary affiliation, training, and other factors, are congruent with the innovation, and/or if supervisors receive adequate training to understand the philosophy and behaviors specific to the innovation. Further, it is necessary for supervisors' expectations favoring the innovation to be accurately perceived by subordinates, in order for such expectations to influence staff members' role enactment incorporating the innovation.

STANDARD OPERATING ROUTINES

Organizational analysts, especially those using the bureau-cratic-political perspective, have recently renewed emphasis on the importance of standard operating routines for coordinating activities of the many participants in large organizations (March and Simon, 1958; Allison, 1971; Cole, 1979; Sabatier and Mazmanian, 1980; Williams, 1980; Weatherley and Lipsky, 1977). In spite of public outcries at the "insensitivity" of bureaucracies which follow "the rules" in each situation, any large organization must have routines and rules which simplify and regulate the work load for each employee and which coordinate the separate efforts of many employees. Further, much of an employee's work role may consist of learning and following the routines for that position.

However, when a new program is introduced, the old procedures may interfere with, rather than facilitate, appropriate role performance unless detailed analysis examines the entire set of work routines for their degree of conflict or congruence with the innovation. For example, Gross and his colleagues' case study (1971) of an attempted individualized educational program found that the desired flexibility of individual schedules and requirements was hampered by the still-operating school-wide rigid schedules for recess, lunch, and other activities, as well as the standard pupil evaluation system by report cards. In a very different type of program, an attempt to build a model residential community on federal land in Washington, D.C. encountered grave implementation problems partly because the federal agency involved, Housing and Urban Development, had customarily worked through local community agencies; any attempt to develop the project directly, which might have cut through months of negotiations, would have required radical revision of custom and existing routines within HUD (Derthick, 1976).

Several other reports of implementation problems have noted the extensive time and negotiation necessary to create new procedures compatible with the innovative program—for example in the use of time, space, and materials (Emrick and Peterson, 1978; Smith and Keith, 1971), or to "humanize" the intake process for an overloaded social service agency (Hasenfield, 1971). Further, when a new policy is adopted without providing adequate resources for effective implementation, the "street-level bureaucrats" facing a surplus of potential clients often must adopt simplifying routines to help cope with their work load. This tendency is shown well by Weatherley and Lipsky's account (1977) of the impact of a new special education law in Massachusetts, when local educational specialists had to routinize their attempts to provide individual assessment and planning for handicapped children.

A new program may involve one of three kinds of changes in the daily routine of a work unit: (A) the innovation may completely replace previous procedures; (B) it may involve gradual changes to modify procedures, with some old routines dropped as new ones are developed; or (C) the new program may expand existing procedures or add totally new elements to the existing repertoire (adapted from Berman and McLaughlin, 1974). Which type of change is most likely to facilitate implementation is a question rarely addressed in previous studies. An educational change attempt which appeared to emphasize the all-at-once approach is regarded by its analysts (Smith and Keith, 1971) as attempting too much, too fast, in its "alternative of grandeur." Yet, in many organizations a complete over-haul and replacement of existing procedures may be the only way to prevent the existing routines from conflicting with attempts to gradually introduce new procedures. A gradual approach is also likely to lose the momentum necessary for any significant change in day-to-day employee behavior. A program which is perceived as adding to existing work duties, without accompanying changes in work rewards of pay or status, is likely to be resisted by implementing staff, on the grounds that it adds to their work load when they are already fully occupied. Thus, it is hypothesized that program implementation will be most extensive under condition A of a fairly complete and rapid replacement of work procedures, next highest under B, the gradualist approach, and most difficult under C, in which new elements are added to an existing job role. Some additional hypotheses pertaining to routines are that implementation will be facilitated if the work roles contain sufficient standardized procedures to enable predictability of duties from day to day, and if sufficient time and resources are available to analyze and change conflicting procedures.

For fostering long-term change in ponderous organizations, several policy analysts have suggested focusing on organizational componenents which are most crucial to building and maintaining routines—processes of employee recruitment and rewards, information acquisition and dissemination systems, and budgeting (Murphy, 1976; Sabatier and Mazmanian, 1980; Williams, 1980). They suggest that only by attention to these basic support factors can public bureaucracies overcome the short-term, crisis orientation of many political and organizational leaders, to institute widespread organizational changes.

TECHNICAL REQUIREMENTS OF THE INNOVATION

New programs have various characteristics which themselves are likely to influence the processes of implementation. While consideration of the impact of these characteristics might more logically be placed outside this examination of process at several organizational levels, these dimensions are discussed at this point to emphasize their interrelatedness to organizational processes. The *fit* between innovation and the adopting system is hypothesized to be a key factor for the success of implementation efforts.

A number of program dimensions have been identified by previous analysts, particularly those working within the structural analysis or diffusion of innovations perspectives. Programs may differ in the centrality of their focus to the organization's major goals or mission (Greenwood et al., 1975), in their degree of consonance with the rest of the organization's activities, and in their pervasiveness, the percentage of staff members involved in implementing the program (Hage and Aiken, 1970; Beyer and Stevens, 1976). Further, studies from the diffusion of innovations perspective have indicated that the rate of adoption by individuals is positively related to such innovation attributes as its partialization, the extent to which it can be adopted on a trial or piecemeal basis; its communicability, or ease of explanation; and negatively related to the perceived complexity of the innovation (Rogers and Shoemaker, 1971). Programs in client-serving organizations tend to have high centrality, high pervasiveness, and high complexity, but varying degrees of communicability, partialization, and consonance with the adopting organization.

New programs differ in the extent to which their characteristics are specified in advance; some are complete while others leave details to be created by the implementor. An example of a fully specified innovation is the introduction of a new drug to the medical community for which appropriate uses, dosages, and likely side effects have been developed in advance by the required pharmacological testing. In contrast is dissemination of educational programs stressing individualized or "open" classrooms, in which the teacher is introduced to broad, philosophical guidelines about how children are expected to learn and then left to develop the details of actual daily interaction in the classroom.

This distinction is similar to Yin's (1980) comparison of "task-specific" versus "task-diverse" technological innovations.

A task-specific innovation serves a single, specific function within the adopting agency; for example, the use of breath-testing instruments by police to test for intoxicated drivers. A task-diverse innovation can be used for a variety of applications, sometimes for both service delivery and administrative functions, such as the introduction of a computer system to a police department.

Several researchers have found the lack of behavioral specification of the "program" in question to be a major barrier to implementation (Berman and Pauly, 1975; Lukas, 1975). Further, an evaluation of educational "project information packages" found a strong tendency for adopters to implement with greater fidelity highly explicit procedures (from information kits about educational projects developed in other school districts) than loosely specified guidelines (Campeau et al., 1979).

Others believe, however, that a new program involving changes in interpersonal roles should not be fully specified in advance as if it were a new drug or machine. To the extent that the program developer attempts to behaviorally specify the exact procedures to be followed in an interpersonally innovative program, the active participatory involvement of the implementators, apparently necessary for role learning, might not occur (Fairweather et al., 1974; Fullan and Pomfret, 1977). For this reason, the extensive Rand Corporation Study of implementation in education concluded that successful implementation must be a process of mutual adaptation between local users and program characteristics (McLaughlin, 1976).

Noting this distinction in technical requirements of an innovation, Fairweather and his colleagues hypothesized (1974) that appropriate communication media for introducing different types of innovations will differ. If the innovation involves little change in role specification or normative behavior, a communication method reaching a large audience but of limited intensity (such as a brochure or the mass media) is likely to be appropriate. But if the innovation involves radical changes in role behaviors, or if the adopting unit is a cohesive social group within an organization, then a communication of more limited scope but of high intensity (for example, a face-to-face workshop) is likely to be needed. This thesis was strongly supported by an experimental comparison (Fairweather et al., 1974) of written versus workshop communications to stimulate decisions to accept a community-oriented lodge program among 255 state mental hospitals.

A similar hypothesis can be proposed for the continuing implementation of a program in which details, such as role changes, must be worked out by the implementors. In this case, information transmittal alone, such as introductory training sessions or technical manuals, will not be sufficient to ensure implementation. Instead, continuing problem-solving sessions will be necessary to facilitate mutual adjustment of the program's details with the social system implementing it. This hypothesis receives support both from Fairweather and associates' (1974) examination of a written technical manual versus active consultation as facilitators of mental hospitals' attempts to implement the lodge innovation, and from the survey of 681 teachers in innovative educational programs conducted by the Rand Corporation in which frequent problem-solving meetings, especially those connected with local development of teaching materials, were a major factor associated with higher program implementation (Berman and Pauly, 1975; McLaughlin, 1976).

COMMUNICATION FLOW

The preceding discussion of technical requirements of the innovation has introduced the underlying importance of communications within an organization, which refers both to vertical communication between superiors and subordinates—in both directions—and to horizontal interchange between staff members in different departments. "Open" communication channels are considered fundamental by the organizational development theorists; communication mechanisms are also an integral part of studies of diffusion of innovation. But empirical research supports this emphasis on the flow of information for organizational change. Studies of innovative processes among physicians (Counte and Kimberly, 1974), in school districts (Baldridge and Burnham, 1975), in local governmental agencies (Eveland et al., 1977), and in mental hospitals (Fairweather et al., 1974) have found close contact with a source of expertise about the innovation and/or extensive open communication within the organization to be associated with propensity to adopt new programs.

As discussed in the section on macro-level organizational control mechanisms, the widely advocated "participation hypothesis"—that lower-level staff members' participation in decisions facilitates acceptance and implementation of the decision—may have validity because such participation requires open upward communication. Open communication, in turn, can reveal to top-level decision makers the actual working conditions that might counteract implementation, can resolve misunderstandings and fears about the impact of a new program (for example, for job security), and can provide feedback for problem-solving. Open communication systems can also build a group dynamic of commitment to the new program, to develop in staff members the persistance to overcome inevitable implementation problems. The effect of "participation" may thus derive from the availability of an open communication channel rather than from the power of an actual vote in a final decision, although no study available has directly examined this distinction.

Variables relating to the communication patterns within an organization are thus likely to be highly influential in implementing a new program. But not enough empirical evidence is yet available to know whether the key variable is a connection or "bridge" to the source of the innovation (Weikert and Banet, 1976), the extensiveness of contact with the program source or change agent, or simply open communication among the staff members of an adopting unit to promote group morale and facilitate accurate feedback.

WORK GROUP NORMS

Since the findings of work group restrictions on individual workers' output in the Hawthorne studies (Roethlisberger and Dickson, 1939), organizational researchers have recognized the importance of norms within the subunit work group for influencing on-the-job behavior (Blau, 1963; Gouldner, 1954; Katz and Kahn, 1966; Scheff, 1961). For example, a longitudinal panel study of custodial versus treatment-oriented attitudes among mental hospital aides found that in spite of substantial positive attitude change among new employees after a treatment-oriented training period, the new aides rapidly adopted the prevalent attitudes of their ward-level work groups after another six months on the job, becoming much more custodial and authoritarian (Berk and Goertzel, 1975).

Several theoretical perspectives toward organizational change converge on a focus toward the fit between work group norms and the proposed change as an essential element in successful change. Katz and Kahn (1966) detail an example in which the introduction of technically advanced, specialized new machinery into a coal mine was not efficient or profitable until cohesive work groups were reestablished at the primary level. The "diffusion of innovations" researchers also emphasize that the norms of a target group, particularly a traditional or conservative group, strongly influence the likelihood that it will adopt innovations (Rothman, 1974).

A focus on the impact of work group processes has been found important in previous studies of implementation. For example, Weikert and Banet (1976) failed to find outcome differences among three model educational programs, but an analysis of the implementation process among the experimental sites led to the conclusion that how staff members worked together to develop and evaluate their curriculum dominated the outcome of the program. Similarly, Fairweather's analysis of factors relating to successful implementation of a community lodge program for mental hospitals suggested that a cohesive staff group must be formed to push for the innovation, with enough positive group feeling to obtain high morale but enough task-oriented leadership to focus on solving immediate problems (Fairweather et al., 1974). That group dynamics can become destructive if focused on intrastaff conflict and emotionality was also found in some of the hospitals Fairweather studied, as well as in Smith and Keith's (1971) case study of the attempted establishment of an "open" school.

Several hypotheses concerning work group norms can therefore be proposed. For coordination of an innovative program with the rest of the organization, Fairweather's findings suggest that a viable project work group may be an essential element. Within each subunit, it is hypothesized that work group norms of acceptance or rejection of the innovation will influence the level of implementation by individuals. Further, new employees are likely to be socialized into positive or negative beliefs about the innovation by the norms of the already established work group.

In summary, intermediate-level organizational processes described in this section—supervisory expectations, standard operating routines, technical requirements, communication flows, and work group norms—are likely to control the day-to-day pattern of work activities that surround the introduction of a new program or policy. Although the previous perspectives have provided a number of hypotheses about organizational life at this level—particularly organizational development, bureaucratic-political analysis, and, to a lesser extent, structural analysis—the importance of intermediate level processes has been relatively neglected by implementation analysts. Most investigations of implementation have focused either on the political-regulatory context of macro-level change or on the training needs or attitudinal influences of individual implementors.

In the social systems perspective being developed here, intermediate-level processes form the context for the enactment of individual work roles by which an innovation is implemented. Without a work situation compatible with the activities required by the innovation, efforts to change individual staff member's attitudes or behaviors are likely to be frustrated by behavior patterns required by the system of intermediate-level processes. Thus, while individual-level variables are likely to have some significance in implementing new programs, the intermediate-level processes form the immediate social environment within which individuals operate. "The behavior of people in organizations is still the behavior of individuals, but it has a different set of determinants than behavior outside organizational roles" (Katz and Kahn, 1966: 391).

INDIVIDUAL-LEVEL VARIABLES

The third theoretical level of analysis for an examination of implementation is the micro level of individual use: how to obtain from staff members the degree of understanding, commitment, and behavioral change necessary to carry out the innovation appropriately. An enormous literature exists developing various approaches to individual change, with as yet little integration of findings. Several major theoretical approaches were described briefly at the beginning of this chapter within the individual psychology perspective. Since it is not the purpose here to attempt to unsort this tangled web of research, individual-level variables will be analyzed simply in terms of their contribution to role changes required for the implementation of a new program. Several major classes of such variables will be described—behavioral skills, incentives for changed performance, and cognitive supports. These variable classes also derive from the two major branches of psychological change theories: behavioral and cognitive approaches.

BEHAVIORAL SKILLS

Individual variation in implementation may develop, first, from differences in degree of competence in executing the technical skills required for the innovation. Particularly when the technical requirements of the new program are left for specification by the user, individual implementors may or may not fully understand what behaviors are intended by the program designer. Further, even if the level of understanding is high, the users may lack the skills to enact the desired behaviors, especially if the program content calls for changed interactions with a recipient. Such difficulty has been noted in several studies of educational innovations focusing on more individualized teacher-pupil interaction, in which teachers accepted the philosophy underlying an "open education" program but did not know how to create the necessary curricular materials nor how to translate the philosophy into changes in their daily interaction with pupils (Gross et al., 1971; Pincus, 1974; Smith and Keith, 1971; Weikart and Banet, 1975). Similarly, at least one study found pupils equally confused about their new roles as small group participants and directors of their own educational experiences (Smith and Keith, 1971).

Even if the innovation is well specified, learning new role behaviors may require several months of practice. Some skills may be more difficult for implementors to master than others, resulting in uneven initial implementation. These learning processes are noted by diverse sources: an analysis of the gradual diffusion and adoption in the nineteenth century of new industrial technologies, which required factory workers to develop "know-how" on the job (Rosenberg, 1978); and an intensive observational study of teachers learning the separate new skills required by Direct Instruction teaching (Gersten and Carnine, 1980).

The possession of behavioral skills, or the capacity to develop such skills, may be an explanation for the finding within the literature on diffusion of innovations that innovations are more likely to be adopted by those with higher levels of education (Rothman, 1974). Yet, several educational innovation projects cited above found that possession of college or even graduate degrees does not necessarily create the behavioral competence needed to carry out a new program. While those who have shown greater job competence under an existing structure might more easily adopt the behaviors required for a new program, an opposite effect of education might also occur. As Blau (1963) suggests from his intensive examination of the role behavior of federal agents, those with greater existing job competence may derive greater rewards from the existing work structures and thus have little incentive to adopt a new program, to anticipate the variables to be discussed in the next section.

Nevertheless, hypotheses relating to behavioral skill levels can be suggested. Controlling for intermediate-level variables, individual degree of program implementation will be positively related to (a) higher education levels, in general; (b) education which relates directly to the program being introduced, such as psychology courses for a psychology-derived therapeutic program in a mental health facility; (c) a longer time period for attempting to use the innovation, during which behavioral skills may be developed by trial and error, and (d) a longer, more intensive training program in the use of the innovation. This last hypothesis on length of training is very speculative, because the value of a training program may depend more on the extent of its focus on behavioral skills than on length of training per se.

INCENTIVES

Recent behavioral theory in social psychology has placed renewed emphasis on the individual's motivation for performing learned behaviors or the structure of rewards and costs which follow a behavior. Similarly, organizational analysts have long been studying the effects on worker motivation of changes in a pay system, such as piecework or group incentives (reviewed by Melcher, 1976; Lawler, 1976). From these studies has emerged the conclusion that many workers' motivation is not a simple direct function of rates of pay but may also involve such factors as acceptance into a supportive work group, legal-like compliance with legitimate authority, and satisfactions from the work itself or from accomplishments within it (Kalleberg, 1977; Katz and Kahn, 1966).

Which of these motivational structures is likely to enhance implementation of a new program is an open question with little previous research. Several case studies of educational change noted problems with an apparent lack of the motivation among teachers to make extra efforts needed for implementing the innovation (Gross et al., 1971 ; McLaughlin, 1976). A synthesis of findings from five studies of educational change concluded that mutual self-interest and social interaction with change agents were more powerful motivations for individual change than perceived needs or problem-solving (Emrick and Peterson, 1978). Yet, little firm evidence is available to distinguish whether the appropriate incentives would be colleague approval, tangible rewards provided by the organization, or evidence of higher pupil achievement. Further, since many human service innovations are undertaken in public bureaucracies with predetermined civil service pay and promotion schedules, the organization may have few tangible rewards to offer for extra effort devoted to change.

Another complication in studying workers' incentives for adopting change is that individual staff members may differ in their work orientations. A basic distinction can be typified by the phrases "having a job" versus "building a career." For the jobholder, orientation is toward doing a fair days' work to bring home a paycheck, following what is expected by the supervisors, and getting along well with co-workers, without much personal concern for accomplishing goals, viewed to be the responsibility of the supervisory level. In contrast, a person motivated toward career-building may be rewarded by the job accomplishments that a new program could contribute, as well as the professional recognition derived from being "an innovator." This may be an explanation for previous findings that those motivated by "professional concerns" are likely to be receptive to innovations (McLaughlin, 1976), while lower-level organizational members, more likely to be jobholders, are seen as more resistive to change (Rothman, 1974). Further, new programs which require that implementors create the technical details for application are likely to provide an arena for accomplishment by the career builders, while jobholders would more readily implement a program in which details are spelled out and integrated with their other work routines. If, as is likely, many innovative human service programs are presented to organizations dominated by jobholders, rather than first developed in detail by career builders, worker motivation may be incongruent with the requirements of the innovation at that particular stage of its development.

Hypotheses about incentives for individual staff members to undertake the behavioral changes needed to implement a new program are thus very tentative, since little is known about what particular rewards will motivate changed behavior of staff members with varying orientations. Certainly the professionalism hypothesis needs further testing: Do "professionally oriented" workers tend to implement innovations more readily? Does this tendency interact with the technical requirements of the new program, as suggested above? Further, the number and intensity of problems associated with the innovation, viewed as an index of disincentives or costliness of the program, is likely to be negatively related to individual implementation.

Feedback of data from clients showing positive results of the program may stimulate fuller implementation by staff motivated toward goal accomplishment, although unambiguously positive effects are not common evaluative outcomes. Performance feedback on the level of implementation itself, especially if made public, may have a powerful effect on workers. This was shown by Quilitch's investigation (1975) of three staff-management procedures for stimulating ward workers to lead recreational activities in an institution for the retarded. In this investigation, neither a memo from the chief administrator nor an inservice workshop on recreational activities led to any increase in ward activities, but assigning staff as activity leaders and posting performance feedback increased the level of such activity by over 400 percent.

Whether or not overall job satisfaction (a measure of overall rewards from the job) would be positively reated to individual implementation is difficult to predict, since findings on the relationship between job satisfaction and productivity are mixed but generally do not show a strong association (Quinn et al., 1974). On the other hand, a moderate to high level of satisfaction with one's work may be necessary to generate the extra effort, the risk-taking, that is involved in committing oneself to a new program.

COGNITIVE SUPPORTS

The influence of individual cognitions such as beliefs, attitudes, felt needs, and perceived choices in relation to behavioral change has been extensively studied but remains a controversial area of social psychology (Kiesler et al., 1969; Schuman and Johnson, 1976). Certainly the view that persuasive communication to change beliefs and attitudes toward an innovation is all that is needed to ensure behavioral change is not justified by data from studies of implementation in both mental health organizations (Fairweather et al., 1974) and education (Smith and Keith, 1971). On the other hand, diffusion of innovations researchers have found that innovations whose characteristics match users' "felt needs," as well as recipients without "traditional values," facilitate the acceptance of innovations (Rogers and Shoemaker, 1971).

It may be that attempts to introduce a new program or technique when the implementor's cognitive perceptions about it are negative would generate stressful dissonance between actions and beliefs. While such dissonance might be removed by altering beliefs, particularly if there is open communication and work group support for the innovation, dissonance might also be reduced by not implementing the innovation, or by a pro forma compliance toward implementation. Individual-level resistance to change in preexisting beliefs can have positive functions for an integrated cognitive outlook. For example, if the existing set of attitudes and beliefs provide an informational filter for confirming reality, help the holder to cope with environmental uncertainty, or form the content for a social network of beliefs shared by significant others (Kelman and Warwick, 1973), then the individual is likely to resist accepting communications which threaten this cognitive structure. In sum, cognitive change alone is probably not sufficient to generate individual adoption of a new program, but continuing conflict between implementing staff members' cognitions and the requirements of a new program may be a significant barrier to full implementation.

Several strategies have been suggested by the literature on organizational change which may facilitate cognitive acceptance of new programs. Participation of the ultimate users of an innovation in the decision-making process concerning its adoption, a recommendation which has strong supporters among the organizational development theorists, may be effective primarily because it brings users together to develop social support for the innovation as well as providing information to counter unrealistic beliefs. Further, even the perception of choice may generate personal involvement and commitment to the new program which motivates extra effort toward "making it work." In addition, when participation is accompanied by actual decision-making power, suggested innovations that are perceived too negatively are likely never to receive a favorable decision for initial adoption, thus precluding implementation problems.

A second strategy to reduce cognitive resistance to a new program is the "small change" or "trial" adoption advocated by literature on the diffusion of innovations (Rogers and Shoemaker, 1971), whereby the user can reduce his or her risk of failure, and/or reserve personal judgment, by a small-scale trial of the innovation. For cognitive change, this may be similar to the "foot in the door phenomenon" confirmed by experimental social psychology (Freedman and Fraser, 1966), in which agreement with an experimenter's small initial request is associated with greater willingness to accede to a later, larger request. Thus, if target implementors can try out a new program in their own work situation without a final commitment for adoption, they may see for themselves the program's feasibility and effects, which is likely to overcome many negative cognitions. Further, a trial adoption may enable gradual, and thus easier, behavioral skill learning, if the program is one that can be tried on a partial basis.

Adequate hypotheses to summarize the effects of individual-level cognitive supports on implementing a new program depend on more exact differentiation among types of cognitions. For example, a specific doubt about the likely effect of the innovation might be countered by empirical information on actual tryouts, while a more global attitude toward change in general might be serving as a defensive reaction for anxieties about status or job security and thus be relatively impervious to informational persuasion. Nevertheless, it can be expected that negative cognitions about a program will be associated with more "traditional" job orientations and, in turn, will be related to lower levels of individual implementation. Further, since the social system perspective advocated here emphasizes the influence of the job context on behavior, it is expected that effects of individual-level cognitive variables on implementation will be smaller than effects of the intermediate-level work structure variables already described. However, if intermediate-level pressures for implementation are ambiguous or absent, then individual employees' level of implementation is likely to be positively related to cognitive clarity and favorability toward the new program. Finally, individual cognitions would be expected to be more favorable and level of implementation higher among those staff members who have participated in decision-making regarding the innovation or have had an opportunity to adopt it on a trial basis.

Three levels of analysis for examining implementation processes have now been presented—the macro level of the organization as a whole; the intermediate level of internal structures and procedures; and the micro level of individual skills, incentives, and cognitions. While a number of hypotheses have been suggested relating these variables individually to the degree of implementation, a central thesis of this chapter is that implementation ultimately involves the whole set of processes in interaction as a social system.

In contrast to the six perspectives outlined at the beginning of the chapter, each of which emphasizes one or more important components of the changes involved in implementation, the social systems perspective includes the total set of hypothesized influences within a single framework. This approach is particularly appropriate for applied research addressing real implementation problems, for it incorporates consideration of influences from all the other perspectives, in recognition that the normal caveat of experimental research—"other things being unchanged"—usually does not hold true in applied settings.

In planning research on the organizational changes involved in implementation, one cannot assume that "other factors" will be the same in various organizations; therefore, one should attempt to analyze the variability among the organizational components that are theorized to have relevance for the outcome of interest—in this case, program implementation. Components that have great influence over the success or failure of implementation in one organization at a particular point in time may well be less critical within a different organization, for a different innovation, or even for the same organization at a different point in its evolution or a later stage of the total implementation process. Utilizing a less encompassing perspective for investigation a specific implementation situation might neglect to include the component that was most facilitative—or, as is more often the case, most troublesome—in increasing implementation there.

THE PROCESS OF IMPLEMENTATION OVER TIME: INTERRELATIONS AMONG THE THREE ORGANIZATIONAL LEVELS

The social system perspective utilized here allows simultaneous consideration of the many variables likely to influence program implementation within organizations. At the same time, a synthesis of these parts is needed. Such a synthesis can be built by viewing implementation as a multistage process through which the previously identified components operate to yield successful or unsuccessful outcomes.

Several analysts have suggested that a sequence of stages or subprocesses is useful for examining implementation processes (Yin, 1979; Hall et al., 1977; Eveland, Rogers and Klepper, 1977; Berman, 1980). These writers suggest somewhat different conceptualizations of implementation processes, but share an emphasis on implementation as contingent upon many organizational and individual factors, rather than predictable in advance.

There is thus a growing precedent for treating implementation by time-based process analysis rather than examining this phenomenon purely by cross-sectional data. Although the data presented in Chapters 4 and 5 are cross-sectional, due to the limitations of data collection, the framework is intended to portray a dynamic system that is constantly changing.

Implementation is here conceptualized as a five-stage process, although these "stages" might well overlap each other in time. Further, the sequence might unfold without change at each stage necessarily being successful before the next stage is begun. Figure 2.1 diagrams this five-stage process; arrows indicate relationships among the organizational components already described. Arrows in the diagram are intended to be tentative; the types and directions of influence in a complex social system are, in reality, likely to be fluid and somewhat unique to each situation.

The program initiation stage is the *decision to adopt,* during which the decision-making components issue a more or less authoritative decision to undertake, or at least to try out, the innovative program. The decision to adopt typically involves the macro-level components most heavily; that is, environmental pressures, interests of organizational participants, and the normal organizational control processes are influential at this point to determine what type of program, if any, will be adopted. Such decision processes also incorporate the organization's major purposes for the innovation—that is, whether aims are largely symbolic or for goal attainment.

The heart of the implementation process involves three stages: *assembling resources, role change,* and *problem-solving.* While these appear in a diagram as roughly sequential, they are probably overlapping and mutually contingent—the resources needed depending somewhat on the extent of role change, role change processes depending on time and personnel resources available, and the extensiveness of problem-solving depending on the outcomes of the first three stages—and in turn likely to stimulate recycling organizational activity back through these stages. Assembling resources includes securing needed financial and physical facilities for the new program, hiring new personnel or reassigning present employees to it, and (a resource which

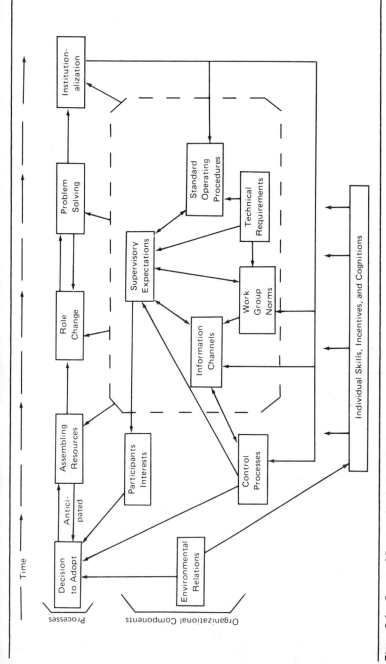

Time

Institution-
alization

Problem
Solving

Role
Change

Assembling
Resources

Anticipated

Decision
to Adopt

Participants
Interests

Supervisory
Expectations

Standard
Operating
Procedures

Technical
Requirements

Work
Group
Norms

Information
Channels

Control
Processes

Environmental
Relations

Individual Skills, Incentives, and Cognitions

Processes

Organizational Components

Figure 2.1: Stages of Program Implementation

is often overlooked) allowing adequate time for putting in place the changes mandated by the new program. Role change focuses on the actual behavior of implementing staff members, the fit between the new behaviors and the expectations of supervisors and co-workers, and the degree of consonance or conflict with other normal work routines of implementing staff members. Including problem-solving as the fourth explicit stage in the implementation process emphasizes the contingent nature of organizational relationships. Even with careful prior planning, the success of implementation attempts cannot be guaranteed; feedback for problem-finding and diagnosis is likely to suggest further modifications of resources and roles before the innovation becomes a part of the normal organizational routine.

In the diagram shown in Figure 2.1, the intermediate-level components are grouped together within a dotted circle to indicate that they are all likely to influence the three key stages: assembling resources, role change, and problem-solving. In addition, they influence each other and so are diagrammed with double-headed arrows between them. Therefore, the influence of each component for overall implementation progress may operate both directly on each stage of the process and indirectly by influencing other intermediate-level components.

For example, supportive supervisory expectations are hypothesized to be a direct facilitator of appropriate role change. In addition, supervisory expectations are likely to have indirect influence on such role changes by helping to establish congruent standard operating routines, by maintaining open communication channels, and by charismatic influences on work group norms. Similarly, the mechanisms established and/ or supported by supervisors for problem-solving, or the lack thereof, will greatly facilitate or impede this stage in the total process. Thus, Figure 2.1 does not include all the arrows linking each intermediate-level component with each of the middle three stages, for the diagram would become unnecessarily cumbersome. In addition not enough evidence is yet available to determine the relative strengths of these direct and indirect influences at different stages of the total implementation process.

The fifth stage is institutionalization, or embedding the innovation into the normal operating routines. If the preceding stages have been successful, new roles and structures should have been created so that the extra resources and special problem-solving mechanisms can be removed or lessened without the collapse of the innovation. Thus, institutionalization is conceptualized as an organizational equilibrium point, but even new programs which are eventually well implemented may require several years before reaching this point. Many other programs never officially terminated also may never engender much behavior change among the supposedly implementing staff members. In addition, other organizational problems or programs are likely to engulf the organization before the implementation of any one program is institutionalized, so this stage does not imply that the organization as a whole is "in equilibrium."

In this overview of processes comprising implementation, the idea of role change becomes the key linking concept between levels of analysis. Individual staff members' behaviors are viewed as products of both their own backgrounds of skills and cognitive role definitions and the context of expectations from supervisors and co-workers. Yet, as Graen's research on role-making has emphasized (Graen, 1976; Haga et al., 1974), organizational roles are most realistically portrayed not as fixed bureaucratic slots but as dynamically constructed results of negotiation between each incumbent and his or her role partners. When an organizational decision stimulates genuine efforts to implement a new program, then the role change necessary for one level of participant is likely to require reciprocal role changes from role partners such as supervisors, who in turn may need to renegotiate their roles with central administrators, and so forth. The resulting personal stress and tension as such role negotiations are conducted is often termed "role conflict."

Several previous studies have found that occupants of innovative positions in organizations tend to exhibit higher levels of personal role conflict (Kahn et al., 1964; Miles and Perreault, 1976; Rogers and Molnar, 1976). These findings lead to the hypothesis that efforts to implement a new program within a complex bureaucratic organization will result in higher levels of individually felt role conflict. Since role conflict is by definition a state of tension and stress, individual staff members may seek to resolve it by avoiding the changes required for implementation. Thus, unless there is a source of pressure and support for change coming from outside the ongoing work situation to stimulate the necessary series of role renegotiations, implementation is likely to be pro forma at best. The ongoing social system will prevail if insufficient resources are available to pay the costs of change.

In conclusion, this review has brought together into one organizational model the major strands of theory and research which illuminate the overall problems of program implementation. By examining organizational processes at three levels of analysis—the macro level of the organization as a whole; the intermediate level of subunit processes; and the micro level of individual behaviors, incentives, and cognitions—this chapter has developed the theme that implementation must be considered a problem involving the whole organizational social system. Table 2.2 summarizes the components and preliminary hypotheses which constitute the framework.

Although previous empirical work has not often been conducted within this perspective, the studies reviewed here do reveal considerable support for the overall conclusion that each of the component processes can be a vital influence on implementation success or failure. Yet, the many hypotheses raised, their tentative nature, and the sometimes conflicting hypotheses derived from different sources reveal the limitations and gaps in the body of previous empirical research on implementation.

In view of the complexity of implementation as a research problem, it is probably inevitable that no one empirical study could incorporate all the potentially relevant variables or hypotheses. The organizational framework of implementation developed here is thus not meant to be directly testable as a single mathematical model. Instead, it has been developed as an integrating and summarizing conceptual model of previous literature, an overview of organizational factors to be examined by program managers facing implementation problems, and a stimulus for continued empirical research.

TABLE 2.2
Summary and Hypotheses:
Analytical Framework for the Study
of Social Program Implementation

Central hypothesis: Differential degrees of implementation of an innovative social program are best explained by the organizational context in which the implementors work. Neither characteristics of the setting nor characteristics of the individuals alone enable as adequate an explanation as both types of variables considered together.

I. *Macro-Level Components* this level of analysis focuses on the organization or implementing system considered as a whole (e.g., the school district).

  A. Decision processes: Who is involved in the decision to adopt the innovative program and what are their stakes?

    Hypotheses

      Implementation will be facilitated if:

        (a) influential decision makers are oriented toward problem-solving rather than toward personal or organizational opportunity;

        (b) those influential in the decision to adopt are in high enforcement positions (i.e., "line administrative relationship") over those implementing the program.

  B. Control processes: How do the normal supervisory and coordinating mechanisms (e.g., centralization versus decentralization of decision-making, enforcement of rules, etc.) relate to the innovation?

    Hypotheses

      Implementation will be facilitated if:

        (a) those responsible for implementing an innovation are able to participate in the decision regarding its adoption;

        (b) central administrators strongly and actively support the program;

        (c) the degree of user autonomy characteristic of the innovative program (see "technical requirements of the innovation") is congruent with the usual control process within the organization.

  C. Obtaining resources: How adequate are the financial support, number of staff members, and the amount of time (considered both as time in the daily schedule and as the number of months necessary for full implementation) available to support implementation?

    Hypotheses

        (a) Adequate financial and staff resources to carry out a program are important components for implementation, but increasing staff or funding alone are not sufficient to bring about change.

        (b) Implementation will be facilitated if planning and preparation time is incorporated into the users' routine schedules, and into the longer-term expectations for results from the innovation.

(Continued)

TABLE 2.2 **(Continued)**

(c) The more resources are obtained outside the organization's usual sources of support, the more difficult will be long-term implementation.

D. Relationships with the environment: How favorable is the operating context of beneficiaries, supporters, competing services, and regulators?

Hypotheses

(a) Environmental influences from beneficiaries, supporters, competing services, and regulators can support or undermine implementation.

(b) The more diverse the external coalition supporting the initiation of a social program, the easier will be the political processes leading to adoption of the program, but the more difficult implementation becomes.

(c) The larger the body of regulations affecting a particular organization, the more difficult is implementation of a particular innovative program.

II. *Intermediate-Level Processes*—this level of analysis focuses on the subunits within an organizational system, such as schools within a school district or wards within a hospital.

A. Supervisory expectations: What role expectations for subordinates within a work division are communicated by the supervisor of the division?

Hypotheses

Implementation will be facilitated if:

(a) division supervisors' backgrounds (disciplinary affiliation, training, etc.) and beliefs are congruent with the innovation;

(b) supervisors' expectations favoring the innovation are accurately perceived by subordinates;

(c) supervisors receive adequate training to understand the philosophy and behaviors specific to the innovation, or new supervisory roles are established.

B. Standard operating routines: Are subdivision routines and rules which regulate the flow of work and coordinate various work roles congruent or conflicting with the innovation?

Hypotheses

Implementation will be facilitated if:

(a) the work roles contain sufficient standardized routines to enable predictability of duties from day to day;

(b) necessary changes in work duties are undertaken completely and rapidly, rather than gradually changed or added to existing work duties.

TABLE 2.2 (Continued)

C. Technical requirements of the innovation: Are characteristics of the program fully specified in advance or are details left to be created by the implementor?

Hypothesis

(a) Appropriate communication and training media for introducing innovations will differ depending on their technical requirements, with programs which incorporate new details created by the users, or which need extensive role changes, requiring active participatory learning.

D. Communication flow: How does information flow in both "vertical" directions (between supervisors and subordinates) and "horizontal" directions (across subdivision boundaries)?

Hypotheses

Implementation will be facilitated if:

(a) there is a higher level of communications of all types within the parts of an organization;

(b) there is a direct source of communication (a "bridge") with the source of the innovation.

D. Work group norms: Are standards of appropriate work behavior that are created by subdivision groups of workers compatible or incompatible with the innovation?

Hypotheses

Implementation will be facilitated if:

(a) there is a cohesive project work group coordinating input from the various parts of an organization which contribute to the program;

(b) subdivision work group norms foster acceptance of the program among individual employees.

III. Individual-Level Variables—this level focuses on the understanding, commitment and behavioral change necessary from individual staff members involved in implementation.

A. Behavioral skills: Do individual implementors possess the behavioral skills required by the innovation, particularly skills for interaction with recipients? Can training develop these skills?

Hypotheses

Individual degrees of program implementation are positively related to:

(a) higher levels of education, in general;

(b) education specifically related to the content of the program being introduced;

(c) longer experience in using the innovation;

(d) longer and/or more intensive training program in the use of the innovation.

(Continued)

TABLE 2.2 (Continued)

B. Incentives: What incentives are available to motivate changed worker behaviors toward implementing the innovation? Do appropriate incentives differ among "jobholders" versus "career builders?"

Hypotheses

    (a) A "professional orientation" toward one's job increases the tendency to implement new programs.

    (b) Individual implementation is positively related to overall job satisfaction.

    (c) The number and intensity of problems associated with a program, viewed as an index of costliness or disincentives, will be negatively related to individual implementation.

C. Cognitive supports: Do individual beliefs, attitudes, felt needs, and so forth that are incongruent with the innovation generate stressful cognitive dissonance between job-required actions and privately held beliefs?

Hypotheses

    (a) Individual implementation is positively related to cognitive clarity and/or to favorability about the program.

    (b) Individual favorability and implementation will be higher among those staff members who have participated in the decision processes surrounding adoption of the program.

    (c) Individual implementation will be higher among implementors who adopt the program on a "trial" basis, with opportunity for feedback of program results.

3

Implementing
Goal Planning

Methods for Study

The social systems model for program implementation developed in Chapter 2 is, of course, a broad overview of the organizational processes likely to influence success or failure in the adoption of innovative social programs. The literature potentially applicable to this applied research topic yields a wide variety of interconnected hypotheses with varying degrees of empirical support.

The research reported in the remainder of this book is an exploration of the fit between this analytical model and data concerning implementation behaviors in two mental health facilities, both state-financed institutions in upstate New York. Since only two nonrandomly chosen organizations are studied, no statistically validated generalizability to other organizations is intended. Instead, the focus of this research was to examine the total set of organizational variables surrounding implementation in the two facilities, and particularly in the Developmental Center, to collect extensive enough data to test quantitatively some of the previously derived hypotheses concerning intermediate and micro-level processes. This chapter will therefore describe the methods of data collection and analysis for the more extensive research project at the Developmental Center. Chapter 5 will describe the more qualitative research methodology for the Psychiatric Center.

THE SETTING

The Developmental Center is a New York State Department of Mental Hygiene residential facility for developmentally disabled and mentally retarded individuals—both children and adults. It forms the central administrative core for a network of regional centers and family care homes promoting community-based services for the developmentally disabled in six counties in the Southern Tier of New York. The Center opened in fall 1974 and was still growing in numbers of both residents and staff when this study was conducted. By fall 1977, when data for this study were collected, it housed about 190 residents, half of them children and adolescents. Since the center was built to house approximately 500 residents, new residential units were regularly opened. In fall 1977, therapeutic staff numbered 159 nurses, therapy aides and ward aides, plus about 40 staff members in support departments such as psychology, social work, education, children's habilitation, speech and hearing, physical and occupational therapy, and vocational rehabilitation. Physically, the center is an interconnected series of one- and two-story grey brick buildings which spread over and around a hilltop in a semirural area.

The developmentally disabled residents of the center live in "units" (wards), each housing 20 to 24 persons of about the same age and developmental level. The physical facilities for each of the center's nine units include a large living-dining area, three play or TV areas, bedrooms for each one or two residents, bathrooms, a nursing station with a treatment-records room, and a small staff lounge and storage area. Working with the residents on each unit during three daily work shifts are two to four nurses, who are overall supervisors of the unit's activities; 12 to 16 therapy aides; and two ward aides responsible principally for cleaning and maintenance. The residents living in each unit spend much of their time during a typical weekday going to various program areas, which are administratively separate departments of the center. Program areas examined for this study include Children's Habilitation (CH) which does mostly one-to-one behavioral teaching of preacademic and daily living skills; Special Education, whose teachers focus on academic and preacademic training with small groups of children; Speech and Hearing, which provides language acquisition programs and hearing evaluations in individual sessions; Occupational and Physical Therapy, also offering one-to-one therapy primarily for physical development and mobility; and Vocational Rehabilitation, which provides simulated workshop and home living settings for orienting adult residents toward work activity.

Therapy aides working in the residential units are ideally both first-line care givers and teachers of basic skills in daily living. They are responsible for dressing, bathing, feeding, administering medications and any other needed nursing activities, as well as attempting to teach daily living skills and to follow behavioral techniques for correcting problem behaviors. They also take residents to and from the program areas, and sometimes engage in recreational activities with them. Each therapy aide is a primary therapist for three to five residents, meaning he/she is responsible for their scheduling, clothing, and general supervision, although the primary therapist does not necessarily do all the care-taking for "his/her primaries." The residential unit is thus the home base for the residents living there, with specialized staff in the program areas providing intensive therapy and teaching.

THE INNOVATION

The program studied is a therapy-planning and record-keeping system called the Generalized Goal Planning System. It was devised with federal grant support by the present chief psychologist at the center while he was in a previous position in another state. The central elements of the system are (1) a behavioral approach toward planning each therapeutic intervention, the Goal Plan, and (2) standard written formats for records of Goal Plans undertaken and for periodic progress reports called Milestones. Written documents explaining the Goal Planning approach (Findikyan et al., 1975; Houts and Scott, 1975) emphasize that all treatment objectives for the developmentally disabled can and should be specified as observable behaviors to be attained by individual clients within a specified time. Intervention methods to help the client reach the specified goal are to be clearly articulated in the form of procedural steps. The actual methods used for any particular Goal Plan need not be the procedures typically used in behavior modification, but might include group interaction, community activities, or medication, so long as the procedural steps are explicitly related to an observable goal in precise enough language that a new therapist, for example, could pick up the Goal Plan and follow it.

The written form on which Goal Plans are to be recorded was devised for both the therapist's use and for computer processing. It includes spaces for precoded and for written entries specifying the problem, the goal to be attained, the client's present skill or behavioral level, intervention method(s), current and target dates, names of implementor(s) and their program supervisor, and a schedule for exact times when the intervention is to be undertaken. A separate form is provided for monthly "Milestone" progress reports for each Goal Plan in effect. (Sample copies of these forms appear in the appendices.)

Goal Planning was begun at the Developmental Center with the arrival of the chief psychologist in spring 1975, soon after the center opened. Interviews with senior staff indicate there was very little controversy about whether or not to adopt Goal Planning. Since the State Department of Mental Hygiene was requiring some form of goal-oriented treatment planning, this system met state requirements. The deputy director-clinical simply issued an interstaff memo adopting Goal Planning as official policy. However, it did not replace any other type of medical records then in use, but was added to numerous types of records also being maintained. The implications of this decision-to-adopt process will be further discussed in Chapter 4.

Training was given to most staff already hired, and several days' orientation to Goal Planning has been included in the six-week training period for therapy aides, ward aides, and nurses hired since then. Thus, for most staff, implementation of Goal Planning has not formally required a change of on-the-job behavior, since it has been official policy since their arrival. But, as the data to be presented will indicate, the extent and distribution of actual implementation of Goal Planning reveals that official adoption of a program does not ensure its implementation.

The present study was initiated through contact with the chief psychologist in the summer and fall of 1976. He provided introductions to the heads of the various departments at the center and remained the principal facilitator of data collection within the center. Interviews with 13 senior-level staff in February 1977 gave an overview of the center's programs, organization, and personnel. With permission from the center's Research Committee, a pilot study undertaken in one residential unit in spring 1977 included examining Goal Planning records and interviewing unit staff about their work roles and their perceptions of Goal Planning. When the results of this pilot study indicated that a larger-scale study was administratively feasible and would yield substantial data about the organizational context of implementation, the present investigation was undertaken. The center's Medical Care Evaluation Studies Subcommittee of the Utilization Review Committee (responsible for overview of therapeutic programs) gave permission for the study. A report of the findings was also submitted to the New York State Department of Mental Hygiene, to help fulfill a state requirement for each mental health facility to undertake several "Medical Care Evaluation Studies" each year. Apparently, all therapeutic efforts are officially seen as a part of a center's "medical care." While conducting the study, I was designated an "Intern in Program Evaluation Research," with office space and informal affiliation with the center's Psychology Department.

GOAL PLANNING DATA

Data to construct the dependent variables for this study were collected from the center's records for each resident within five of the center's nine units. The records notebook for each resident contains the case history, medications reports, legal documents, clothing inventories, and so on, as well as the Goal Plans and monthly Milestone reports. Goal Plans were examined for each target resident for the 14-month period preceding this study, from September 1976 through October 1977.

Information from each Goal Plan that was coded for this study included the resident's unit and individual identification number; the date and type of goal; a code number for the staff member who wrote the plan and for any additional staff who had signed the plan as implementors; a rating for observability and specificity of the goal and plan; and information on the number, dates, writers, and content of the Milestone reports. Each plan's status at the time of coding was recorded: indicating whether the plan had been completed or not; if completed, whether successfully meeting the goal or not; if not yet completed, whether Milestone reports were up-to-date or not. Finally, a brief list of the resident's problems and deficits as determined by the most recent staff conference was made, although these data were not included in the data set for computer processing. All information on the Data Plan Code Sheets, except the problem and deficit lists, was recorded by numerical codes devised in advance, so the code sheets were immediately ready for keypunching. A sample code sheet is in Appendix B.

Coders for the Goal Plan data were the author and two paid assistants, one an undergraduate psychology student and the other a recently graduated psychology major who was available for this part-time work. Both coders had already worked within the center as volunteers or part-time therapy assistants and so were familiar with the Goal Plan system, but were not working with the target units or residents. Training for the coders was provided by the author, who was also present during the coding work periods to discuss and resolve any questions of the appropriate category for a particular item.

Reliability estimates for the coding of Goal Plan information were obtained by duplicate, independent coding by a second coder of records for approximately 20 percent of the residents of each unit. The records to be recoded were chosen via a table of random numbers. The original and duplicate codings for each Goal Plan were then compared for any differences in the exact scoring of individual entries. An "entry" is any item recorded on the Goal Plan Code Sheet; the number of entries differs among Goal Plans because the number of monthly Milestones or of "other implementors" differed. A reliability coefficient for each unit and for all units together was then computed using the formula

$$R = \frac{\text{(number of entries in agreement)}}{\text{(total number of entries.)}}$$

The overall reliability coefficient obtained, .82, indicates that more than 80 percent of all entries checked were coded exactly the same by two coders. Data on the reliability checks for each unit is presented in Table 3.1. (Unit 1 had fewer cases recoded because nine of its 22 residents had no Goal Plans at all.) The number of Goal Plans written by an individual staff member, the entry mainly used as a dependent variable, would in fact have much higher coding reliability, for only two plans were found by one coder but not by the other, and only three cases of different coding of the Goal Plan writer occurred in the 64 Goal Plans checked.

The difficulties of obtaining reliable coding of Goal Plans reflect a number of problems in using official records as a measurement of implementation. One source of problems was the state of the medical record notebooks themselves. Particularly the Milestone reports, which were supposed to be attached to the back of the appropriate Goal Plan, often were not attached to any Goal Plan or even were attached to the wrong

TABLE 3.1
Reliability Data for Goal Plans

UNIT	Number of Resident cases Re-coded	Number of Goal Plans Total	Total Number of Entries	Mean Entries Per Goal Plan	Number of Differences in Coding	Mean Number of Differences Per Goal Plan	Reliability By Unit
1	3	11	163	14.8	21	1.91	.8712
2	5	11	158	14.4	28	2.55	.8228
3	4	13	173	13.3	34	2.62	.8053
4	4	15	252	16.8	53	3.53	.7896
5	5	14	239	17.1	43	3.07	.8201
TOTAL	21	64	985	15.4	179	2.80	.8183

plan. Coders were instructed to try to connect Milestones to the correct Goal Plan using type of goal, dates, and the program location of staff members signing each as clues to correct placement. Yet, the resulting judgments about such placements were not always replicated by a second coder, thus lowering the reliability coefficient.

A second and potentially more serious problem is the extent to which Goal Plans written were not in the records' notebooks at all. This could happen legitimately when outdated plans (and other records) were sent to the Medical Records Department for permanent storage. In this case, the resident's record was supposed to include a summary list of the title and dates of plans sent to Medical Records, but it is unknown to what extent the summaries were accurate. When a summary list indicated that Goal Plans written within the target period had been sent to Medical Records, or a therapy aide or other source mentioned additional plans that might be there, the Goal Plans were searched for in Medical Records and, if located, coded. But it is possible that additional plans had been written and then sent to Medical Records without leaving a "trace" of their existence, and thus were not included here. However, more than a dozen individual records were checked in Medical Records without finding additional previously unrecorded Goal Plans. The operational definition of the implementation of Goal Planning is therefore derived from the Goal Plan records that could be traced. This definition is not only indicative of the practical data collection problem but also reflects the records that would be available to a new staff member attempting to find out what Goal Plans had been tried in the past for a particular resident.

The problems encountered in attempting to obtain accurate, objective data on the extent of Goal Planning by individual staff members may be a source of information about the staff's orientation toward Goal Planning. As Garfinkel (1967) has pointed out, there may be "good" organizational reasons for "bad" institutional records, especially when the person writing the record is not the person using it. When there is little added utility to the record-keeper for increased time and effort devoted to recording information for unknown purposes, re-cord-keeping is likely to suffer. In the case of Goal Planning, the Milestone reports (if done at all) often appeared to be pro forma records, with little utility to the person writing them, who usually knew from personal experience whether the plan was succeeding or not. Since the supervisors, who are nurses, did not feel that overseeing the Goal Planning System was their responsibility, and the small psychology staff did not have time to review record maintenance by individual staff, it probably appeared to many therapy aides that no one noticed or cared whether or not the Milestones were up-to-date or were filed appropriately. Further, the Goal Planning System was not being used as a management information system, as had originally been intended, because the computer facilities and staff were not available. Thus, little systematic follow-up was undertaken of Goal Planning efforts as a whole. In sum, the variable status of record-keeping for Goal Planning was likely to reflect ambivalence within the staff concerning the usefulness of such efforts.

In spite of these problems with collecting objective data about the implementation of Goal Planning, it is likely that the outcome data to be presented here are a reasonably accurate reflection of plans written on the target units over the 14-month period. Obviously, if a therapy aide took the time to write a plan, it was in his/her interest to place it correctly in the records, for potential inspection by supervisors or other therapy aides. Although it is possible that some therapy aides wrote additional plans if they had previously worked on another unit not in the sample of five units studied, this possible source of bias would be very small because only four therapy aides had worked on nonsample units within the 14-month target period.

COMPARISON WITH PREVIOUS MEASUREMENTS
OF IMPLEMENTATION

The data collected for this study from reasonably objective records are likely to present a less biased picture of actual program implementation than the outcome measures for several other recent studies of implementation. Two of the few studies which have undertaken quantitative analyses of similar problems have used interview reports from implementors as the dependent variables (Beyer and Trice, 1978; Berman and Pauly, 1975). For example, in the educational change agent study by the Rand Corporation mentioned in Chapter 2 (Berman and Pauly, 1975), the dependent variables were teachers' and principals' reports of project goals achieved, the degree to which the teachers reported change in their classroom behaviors, and so forth. For a small sample of the change programs studied, additional observations were collected through site visits by the research team. The authors note that the teachers' ratings of percentage of project goals achieved (73 percent) were systematically higher than outside observers' ratings of project success. They justified their continued use of the subjective teachers' data as indicators of implementation on the belief that the upward biases were not systematically related to the predictor variables investigated. Yet, such an assumption is dubious when the organizational pressures to produce a positive external image might also interfere with the trial-and-error processes likely to stimulate genuine implementation.

That interview data are not likely to present highly accurate information on program implementation is shown by a comparison of several sources of data used here. In interviews (methodology to be described below), therapy aides and nurses reported they had written an average of 5.1 Goal Plans per person over the 14-month period. Yet, the data from actual Goal Plan records yielded a mean number of Goal Plans of only 1.6 for the same staff members over the same period. Further, the correlation coefficient between the self-assessed Goal Plan number and the records-derived number is only .53 for these unit staff members, indicating a positive association but not great accuracy of predicting Goal Plan behaviors from interview reports. Thus, the dependent variables to be used here, which derive from objective records of Goal Plans written, are a more accurate reflection of actual program implementation than would be interview reports alone. Since most previous studies of implementation, other than those using interview data, have been case studies not attempting to quantify the relationships examined, the research reported here should reveal a more accurate analysis of implementation processes, within the limited scope of organizations studied.

DEPENDENT VARIABLE CONSTRUCTION

Several potential dependent variables were constructed from the Goal Plans data and examined as measures of individual implementation. The most direct measure used is simply the number of Goal Plans written during the 14-month period. In order to include indicators of other aspects of the Goal Planning System, several indexes were constructed with weighted components for the number of Milestone reports written, the number of plans signed as additional implementors, as well as the number of Goal Plans written. Another variable examined was a dichotomized score of 1 or 0 to indicate whether the staff member had ever written a Goal Plan or not; since 47 percent of the staff had written no plans, this is a measure of any participation in the Goal Planning System. Finally, the staff member's self-assessed report of how many Goal Plans he/she had written during the target period was analyzed against the same set of predictor variables. However, since most analyses revealed very similar results for any of the dependent variables, the discussion of results will focus on the simplest measure: the number of Goal Plans written.

STAFF INTERVIEWS DATA

The major source of information on within-unit organizational characteristics derives from individual interviews with nearly all the staff in contact with the residents of the five units studied, including 51 therapy aides, 14 nurses or supervising therapy aides, 24 staff members of the program departments, and 21 professional and supervisory-level staff.

The five units were selected to exclude two other units which had been opened within six months of the study, most of whose residents were new to the center and whose staff would reasonably not be expected to have undertaken extensive goal planning. Also excluded were a geriatric unit and another adult unit with many older adult residents. Units selected included all three children's units, one adolescent unit, and one unit for fairly high functioning adults who exhibited behavioral problems. Each of the center's two staff psychologists also provided psychological services to at least two of the units in the sample. Thus, the units studied were all housing residents who could be expected to benefit in some degree by systematic therapy planning and were young enough to make an investment of intensive staff time worthwhile, given the limited number of therapeutic staff.

Interviews with nurses, program staff, supervisors, and professional staff were all conducted by the author, usually in the respondent's office, or, for the unit nurses, who had no private offices, in vacant visitor's lounges close to the units. The format for these interviews was semistructured, with some standard questions asked of all respondents in a particular category (for example, nurses) but sufficient flexibility to pursue, as they arose, issues that seemed related to the conceptual model developed in Chapter 2. These interviews were usually one to one and a half hours in length. No staff member at this level refused to be interviewed.

Therapy aides were interviewed by the author (21 interviews) and by two advanced psychology graduate students (15 interviews each), who received graduate study credit for their participation. The interviewers were oriented to the project by discussions with the author and by reading the report of the pilot investigation, which enabled them to follow up appropriately answers to open-ended questions. Additional training activities were discussing in detail the purposes and intent of each interview question and making and then reviewing a videotape of a simulated interview (another graduate student, who was a psychology trainee at the Developmental Center, played the role of a therapy aide for this simulation).

All therapy aides and nurses working on the day or evening shifts of the five units were contacted for interviews, which were completed for all but three of the 68 unit staff (one therapy aide postponed the time for an interview so often that she was perceived to be declining to be interviewed; two other therapy aides were sick and could not be rescheduled during the interview period). The author introduced the project to the staff of each unit or program area, usually in a group meeting. The purposes of the research project were explained as an attempt to understand individuals' perceptions and feelings about their jobs, as well as to explore their perceptions of the Goal Planning System. This explanation did not mention explicitly any attempt to "evaluate" Goal Planning, both because no actual evaluation of outcomes from Goal Planning was included in the research project and because some staff might misinterpret the purpose as evaluating their performance as staff members. The actual interviews were conducted individually, usually in the vacant visitors' lounges near the residential units, for a period of 45 minutes to over an hour. Each interview was preceded by a brief reexplanation of the research project, with assurance of confidentiality. A copy of the explanation of the research project, which was presented conversationally to each respondent, is available in Appendix C, along with a copy of the interview schedule for therapy aides.

The reaction of most staff members to being interviewed was quite favorable; most seemed interested in participating and were open about both positive and negative aspects of their jobs. Many were interested in seeing the results of the study, which were made available to them. Respondent cooperation was generally so positive that the major problem was holding interviews to the scheduled hour.

The interview schedule (see Appendix D) included some open-ended questions, such as a question asking for a general description of job duties to get the respondent talking and to solicit his/her cognitive framework about the job, questions relating to interactions with supervisor and co-workers, and questions on overall orientation and beliefs about the Goal

Planning System. The major portion of the interview focused on structured-response questions about perceptions of time spent and responsibility for a specific list of activities, about frequency of contact with staff in various program areas, about problems and purposes associated with the use of Goal Planning, about training for using Goal Planning, and about background variables such as age, education, and courses in psychology. In addition, each respondent was asked to complete two standard job orientation instruments. One was the Job Descriptive Index (Smith et al., 1968), a measure of satisfaction with the specific facets of one's job, including the work itself, pay, promotions, supervision, and co-workers. The other standard instrument was composed of role conflict and role ambiguity scales designed by Rizzo, House, and Lirtzman (1970)—for this interview, labeled "Job Attitudes Questionnaire." These scales, along with interview items and indexes derived from them, will be described in greater detail in connection with the results for each type of variable.

The assignment of interviewers to interviews was based on their availability at the time the interview could be scheduled, but a strong attempt was made to balance the staff of each unit and each shift across the three interviewers. This attempt was successful, as there were no significant differences by shift or unit in the proportion of interviews conducted by each interviewer. Both dependent and potential independent variables were examined for differences in means by interviewer. Of 40 variables thus examined, four showed means sufficiently different among the three interviewers to be significant at the .05 level, and three others were significantly different with probabilities between .05 and .10. While this degree of difference between interviewers is thus slightly higher than would be expected by chance, it does not indicate substantial interviewer bias.

However, inspection of the mean number of Goal Plans written, a variable not derived from the interview but from the Goal Plan records, revealed fairly large, though not significant, differences by interviewer in number of Goal Plans written (the three means were 1.95, 0.73, and 2.53). Examination of the other variables which showed differences among their means revealed the same ordering of differences as this difference in number of Goal Plans written. Thus, inadvertently there may have been some true differences among the groups of staff interviewed by different interviewers. Whether there was also differential reactivity to the different interviewers is impossible to determine; if present at all, it does not appear to be a large enough effect to influence the results strongly. Since the number of Goal Plans written was not tabulated until after the interviews were completed, and thus was not known to the interviewers, interviewer expectancy could not have influenced interview results.

Data from the open-ended interview questions were coded by the author; coding categories will be described more fully in connection with each variable's results in Chapter 4. A check for reliability of coding was performed by having a second coder rescore the open-ended questions for 30 of the 51 therapy aides interviewed. The correlation coefficients between the two coders for each variable ranged from .63 to .89. Specific reliabilities for each variable are given in Chapter 4. This degree of coding reliability is sufficient for the exploratory purposes of this study.

METHODS OF ANALYSIS

The data from the coded Goal Plans were first examined with the individual plan as the unit of analysis, in order to describe the present extent of the innovation's implementation. Then the frequency counts for interviewed staff on such variables as their number of Goal Plans written, number of Milestone reports, number of completed plans, and number of plans successfully reaching their goal were combined with the coded interview data. The unit of analysis for the major quantitative analyses is thus the level of implementation by individual staff members. Data from the unit staff (both therapy aides and nurses) are usually presented separately from data for staff of the program areas, because their work situations are very different and because those variables derived from the activity list were not available for the program staff (activities within the program areas were all generally treatment-oriented, but differed specifically by discipline).

The major analyses employed multiple regression to examine the influence of the middle-level organizational processes and the micro-level individual variables. As this technique enables examining the explanatory contribution of each independent variable while controlling for the influence of all other independent variables within each equation, the relative influence on Goal Planning of the organizational and individual variables can be compared. In order not to lose scarce degrees of freedom for the analysis of relatively small groups of respondents, missing data were replaced by the mean for that variable, either the total group mean or the mean for that respondents' work location. The handling of missing data will be further described in connection with the construction of each independent variable.

Finally, exploration of the macro-level components of the model, as they influenced the development of Goal Planning, was derived from the qualitative examination of interviews with professional staff, program supervisors, and senior administrators, in addition to inspection of relevant documents. Several of these persons were interviewed twice; a total of 30 interviews were conducted with 21 different persons. The focus of this effort was to develop a case study of the processes surrounding the adoption and continued operation of Goal Planning. The interviews at this level were conducted by the author; open-ended questions focused on the issues which were hypothesized to be influential at the macro level. Notes were written during the interview, which were expanded into as much detail as could be recalled as soon as possible after the interview. Written documents examined included the center's Policies and Procedures Manual, Personnel Office documents, and several unpublished papers on goal planning. In addition, the comments and replies to open-ended questions from the interviews with lower-level staff were reviewed for their contributions to the macro-level issues. These interview materials will also provide illustrative examples for the quantitative findings at the middle and micro levels.

4

Implementing
Goal Planning

Results

The Goal Plan system for planning, recording, and following up treatment interventions was introduced to the Developmental Center in the spring of 1975. By fall 1977, when the data reported here were collected by the methods detailed in Chapter 3, staff members' overall reactions to Goal Planning ranged widely. When asked what she thought of Goal Planning in general, one nurse exclaimed,

> It stinks! The therapy aides frustrate themselves and the residents by trying to teach things that these residents can't learn.

In contrast, one therapy aide's assessment was,

> Goal Plans are the only way they will learn. It sometimes takes six to eight months of work on one plan, but they usually do learn the skill.

This chapter examines briefly the extent to which Goal Planning had been implemented by fall 1977 in the units and program areas studied and by the individual staff members interviewed. Then the analytic model developed in Chapter 2 is

applied to this situation, to assess its utility toward an explanation of variations in individual level of Goal Planning.

IMPLEMENTATION OF GOAL PLANNING, SEPTEMBER 1976-OCTOBER 1977

The data collected from the residents' medical records notebooks yielded a total of 389 Goal Plans written for residents of
the five units during the 14-month period. Table 4.1 shows the
overall total and status of these plans at the time of coding for
each unit and program area. The differential numbers of plans,
shown in column 5, reveals that the overall use of Goal Planning
by most work units is rather low, with the exception of the
Children's Habilitation (CH) staff. Among the residential units,
even the highest total, 35 Goal Plans for Unit 5, is an average of
only 2 and one-half plans written during each month of the
14-month target period, while the lowest total, for Unit 1,
represents just over one plan per month. In terms of plans per
resident, with 20 to 24 residents on each unit, an average of
little more than one plan per resident had been written by staff
during this period. Tabulation of types of Goals (not shown
here) revealed that unit staff tended to focus on procedures for
reducing or eliminating problem behaviors (40 percent of the
137 plans written within the units) and on daily living skills,
such as self-feeding, dressing, and toileting (38 percent of the
total).

Among the program areas, only Children's Habilitation was
using Goal Planning fully at the time of this study; the staff in
this discipline had written 121 plans for residents within the
target units. For all the program areas, the data shown here
reflect their Goal Plans only for the target units, not for
residents from other units or outpatients, who were also receiving services from these program areas. All the Education
Department Plans were written during the 1976-1977 school
year, since the teachers decided to stop using Goal Planning by
fall 1977. In addition, neither Occupational Therapy nor Physical Therapy used the Goal Planning format. The program areas
tended to focus on goals different from the units, for 45

percent of the 252 plans from program areas were for the development of language skills but only 15 percent were for misbehavior correction.

The outcomes for Goal Plans written are revealed by the data on status at the time of coding, given in Table 4.1. That follow-up on Goal Planning was lower than desirable is shown by column 1, which enumerates plans with no Milestones in the records for at least six weeks. These "in limbo" plans were 33 percent of the total overall, but the percentage for several units and programs was substantially higher. Further, an additional 37 percent of the plans had been ended without reaching their goal (column 2); reasons for lack of success included changes in the resident's or staff member's schedule, a frequent happening, or lack of progress toward the goal with subsequent termination or modification of the plan.

Plans whose outcomes were recorded on the Milestones as full or partial successes are enumerated in column 3 of Table 4.1. The overall number of successful plans was just 67, or 17 percent, of the total plans written, but this figure also differs considerably among the units and program areas studied, from a high of 34 percent successful on Unit 5 to only 4 percent terminated as successful in Education and 7 percent in Unit 3. The relatively low number of successful Goal Plans was likely itself to depress staff motivation to continue writing plans, since the plans were not seen to help residents overcome their disabilities. As interview data to be presented below will indicate, belief in the effectiveness of Goal Plans is one variable which relates to increased Goal Plan writing by therapy aides.

Finally, column 4 of Table 4.1 lists plans in progress at the time of coding, with a Milestone written within six weeks or the plan itself having been written within the previous six weeks. As the figures in column 4 are consistently rather low, except for Children's Habilitation, these data indicate the overall low level of Goal Planning being initiated near the end of the 14-month period.

In summary, the data in Table 4.1, on the status of Goal Plans show substantial proportions of Goal Plans left unfinished

TABLE 4.1
Status of Goal Plans by Units and Program Areas

		(1) In "Limbo"— No milestone for 6 weeks or more		(2) Plans ended without success		(3) Plans ended with full or partial success		(4) Plans in progress		(5) Total number of plans	
Units:											
1	N of Plans	5		8		2		0		15	
	%		(33)		(54)		(13)				(100)
2	N	18		4		7		5		34	
	%		(53)		(12)		(21)		(15)		(100)
3	N	21		5		2		2		30	
	%		(70)		(17)		(7)		(7)		(100)
4	N	11		5		5		2		23	
	%		(48)		(21)		(22)		(9)		(100)
5	N	7		10		12		6		35	
	%		(20)		(29)		(34)		(17)		(100)

(Continued)

TABLE 4.1 (Continued)

Programs:		(1) In "Limbo"— No milestone for 6 weeks or more	(2) Plans ended without success	(3) Plans ended with full or partial success	(4) Plans in progress	(5) Total number of plans
Children's Habilitation	N	28	34	29	30	121
	%	(23)	(29)	(24)	(25)	(100)
Education	N	14	68	3	0	85
	%	(17)	(80)	(4)	(0)	(100)
Speech and Hearing	N	14	3	4	5	26
	%	(54)	(12)	(15)	(19)	(100)
Occupational Therapy	N	0	0	0	0	0
	%					
Vocational Rehabilitation	N	10	4	3	0	17
	%	(59)	(24)	(18)		(100)
Psychology	N	1	2	0	0	3
	%	(33)	(67)			(100)
Total:	N	129	143	67	50	389
	%	(33)	(37)	(17)	(13)	(100)

or terminated without progress toward the goal, with smaller percentages either "in progress" or having successfully reached their goal.

Several quality indicators on the uses of Goal Planning are provided by the mean scores listed in Table 4.2. Line 1 refers to the degree to which the goal was an observable behavior of the resident. Observability was coded from 3 for yes, the Goal behavior could be observed, to 1 for no, the Goal was not an observable behavior. As the overall mean of 2.6 indicates, observability was found to be generally high, both overall and among most units. In terms of numbers of Goal Plans, 67 percent (261) of all the plans were given an observability rating of 3, 24 percent (94) were rated 2, or questionable; and only 9 percent (34 plans) were rated 1, or not observable.

Another quality indicator is specificity of the treatment procedure written on the plan. Coders were instructed to use the criterion, "Could you pick up this Goal Plan and follow the treatment procedure indicated?" Again, 3 indicated yes, the treatment procedure was specific, 2 was for questionable, and 1 meant the procedure was not specific enough for an outsider to follow. The overall mean score of 2.6 for specificity, as well as comparably high scores for most units and program areas, again indicates that most plans written were adequately specific. By number of Goal Plans, 65 percent (253) plans were rated 3, or specific; 29 percent (113) were rated 2, or questionable; with only 6 percent (23) rated 1, not specific.

Information about Milestones written is provided by lines 3 and 4 on Table 4.2. The mean number of Milestones per plan was only 1.8, which includes 91 Plans (23 percent of the total) for which no Milestones were written. Further, since the mean time until the final Milestone was 3.7, or nearly four months, it is clear that many plans did not meet the system requirement of at least one follow-up Milestone per month. Yet, the comparatively low number of Milestones means that the paperwork burden for each plan was not excessive; it appears that most plans were deemed a success or failure within two to four months and could be ended.

TABLE 4.2
Mean Scores for Goal Plan Descriptors, by Units and Program Areas

	Mean— all goal plans	UNITS						PROGRAMS			
		1	2	3	4	5	CH	ED	Sp & H	Psyc	VRS
Mean score for observability of goal (Code: 3=yes, (2=?), (1=no))	2.6 (389)	2.7 (15)	2.6 (34)	2.5 (30)	2.8 (23)	2.6 (35)	2.9 (121)	1.9 (85)	2.7 (26)	2.3 (3)	2.8 (17)
Mean score for specificity of treatment plan (Code: 3=yes, (2=?), (1=no))	2.6 (389)	2.5 (15)	2.5 (34)	2.7 (30)	2.8 (23)	2.8 (35)	2.96 (121)	1.9 (85)	2.6 (26)	2.3 (3)	2.8 (17)
Mean number of milestones per goal plan (Number GP's)	1.8 (389)	2.3 (15)	1.9 (34)	.7 (30)	1.7 (23)	1.7 (35)	2.4 (121)	1.4 (85)	1.0 (26)	3.7 (3)	2.1 (17)
Mean time, in months, until final milestone (Number GP's)	3.7 (289) missing=91 or 23%	3.4 (12)	3.6 (22)	2.6 (14)	2.8 (19)	2.4 (25)	3.7 (102)	5.2 (75)	2.5 (14)	1.5 (2)	2.6 (13)

NOTE: Number in parentheses is number of Goal Plans for that cell.

Overall, then, the data in Table 4.2 show that the general quality of Goal Plans written was quite high, in terms of observability of goal and specificity of treatment procedures, but they were not necessarily followed to completion with Milestones. The one program area which tended to have lower scores was Education, which also was the one discipline doing Goal Planning without having had the training sessions to do so. In fact, the teachers were so dissatisfied with the vagueness and lack of specific information in their Goal Plans that they stopped using it by the fall of 1977. In addition, no quality ratings were available for either Occupational or Physical Therapy, since these disciplines had not participated in Goal Planning.

In summary, this data on the quantity and quality of the implementation of Goal Planning leads to the following conclusions: (1) The overall use of Goal Planning by most units and program areas was rather low, with the exception of the Children's Habilitation staff. (2) Follow-up on Goal Plans written was lower than desirable, since 33 percent were in the "limbo" status of late or no Milestones, and few plans included the required one Milestone per month until termination of the plan. It was likely that for many of these plans, the intended treatment procedures were not consistently carried out, resulting in an even lower level of actual therapy than the number of Goal Plans alone would indicate. (3) The proportion of plans which were successful in reaching their goals was relatively low, only 17 percent, which indicates low rates of resident improvement via Goal Planning, and was probably itself a depressant on staff incentive to continue Goal Planning. (4) Quality ratings of the Goal Plans written, for observability of goal and specificity of the treatment procedure, were quite high for most plans. It appears that most staff members knew how to write Goal Plans appropriately, except staff in program areas which had not participated in the training sessions.

CONSEQUENCES OF THE
INTERMITTENT IMPLEMENTATION
OF GOAL PLANNING

It would be ideal at this point to be able to present data showing stronger treatment gains for developmentally disabled residents whose interventions had been developed under a Goal Plan framework than for residents in the same facility without Goal Planning. Such outcome data would present a strong argument that Goal Planning does make a difference, that it ought to be implemented by all staff members. Unfortunately, no such data exist. No experimental evaluation of Goal Planning had been conducted at the Developmental Center, nor at the facility in which it was originally developed. The case for implementation rests on the behavioral principles which inspired the development of the system and on the day-to-day experience of each individual staff member in his/her own work situation. Thus, it is unknown whether fuller implementation of Goal Planning would result in more or faster learning by the residents, or whether it would lead to shorter periods of institutional living before placement in community homes.

In the absence of overall evaluative data on the effectiveness of Goal Plans, a preliminary examination of the usefulness of Goal Planning was attempted by compiling case studies of several individual children on one unit during the pilot phase of this project in early 1977. Staff members in the program areas attended by these children were asked about the treatment activities they were providing, any changes they noticed in children's behavior and capabilities, the records or Goal Plans kept, and their knowledge of the children's activities in other program areas. Several examples from these cases will illustrate some general findings based on these materials. (The individual names, and some typical behaviors, have been changed to preserve confidentiality.)

Harry, age 13, came to the Developmental Center in June 1975 after living in another facility for the mentally retarded for most of his early life. Several misbehaviors which were apparently frequent when Harry first came to the center, such as hitting and biting other residents and staff members, have been controlled, but Goal Plans written for these were not followed up with appropriate Milestones. Harry is able to feed himself and is toilet trained; a problem with nighttime bed-wetting was corrected from June to November 1976 and was appropriately documented with Goal Plans. Staff in Children's Habilitation have been working extensively with him on both receptive and expressive speech by identifying and naming commonly used objects, such as bowl, spoon, and glass. Although Goal Plans on these activities are in his records, neither therapy aide working with him in the residential unit mentioned any attempt to stimulate Harry to use these words appropriately in context during a meal. A previous Goal Plan prepared by the unit staff called for Harry to say the name of a toy he wanted before being allowed to play with it, but this was abandoned when Harry no longer initiated going to the toy room. Unit staff did not mention any other activities to increase his talking, although this was the focus of treatment interventions by both Children's Habilitation and Education.

While both these program areas were emphasizing similar skills for Harry in 1976 and early 1977, especially identifying common objects, staff in each area did not know what the other program was teaching him. The data collected were not detailed enough to tell whether directly conflicting treatments were occurring, but the potential for it was great since both programs were treating the same skill area. Since Children's Habilitation often used food reinforcers to teach specific skills, while the teachers in Education usually did not, it was possible that Harry was supposed to be learning the same behavior under different contingencies in the two programs. Staff members in both areas also mentioned motivational inconsistencies with Harry—"Some days he just will not respond for food reinforcers"—which might have been related to the possible program inconsistency. Neither daytime nor evening staff primary therapists on the unit knew very much about his Goal Plans in

CH or Education; when asked about communication with staff members in these program areas, one therapy aide stated, "Since he has been behaving well lately, there has not been much need for contact with other staff." Thus, Harry's behavior improved since arriving on the unit; he successfully attended programs in CH and Education; but there was little coordination on the content of these programs, nor was there follow-up of skills learned to apply them systematically in a daily living context.

Similar problems occurred in nearly every case examined. For example, Noel, who was 7, had been at the center only about six months and had made substantial progress in learning to feed himself. One unit staff member reported attempts to stimulate him to play with trucks, and diverse activities were provided during his attendance in CH, Education, and Speech; however little of this activity was recorded in Goal Plans, and little coordination was taking place. Staff from all three disciplines mentioned working on eye contact with Noel, again with a strong unrecognized potential for conflicting methods. Several staff also described his apparent refusal to walk correctly from the unit to the program locations, even though he could walk well sometimes. No Goal Plan had been prepared to attempt to correct this; it was likely that each staff member handled it in a different way, with consequent confusion for Noel.

Additional evidence confirming the lack of consistency between disciplines was provided by interviews with two psychologists who had developed detailed case histories of several residents, including observation of their activities in each program area, in fall 1977. Both psychologists mentioned the absence of treatment coordination, and the difficulty of trying to stimulate consistent programs without "stepping on people's toes."

> Staff in [several disciplines] are working on the same types of behaviors. But there are enough differences in techniques to mess up the residents and confuse their learning.

While space precludes further details from individual cases, the same themes occurred in nearly every case. Coordination of activities for the residents was through scheduling times for attending the program areas, with nearly complete autonomy for each program area in objectives and methods to be used. Staff members in all locations seemed to be conscientious, interested in the residents, and dedicated to their work, but no mechanism was being used to ensure continuity or even lack of conflict among the content of the interventions undertaken. Semiannual "staffing" meetings to review the progress of each resident were too infrequent and not connected closely enough with the detailed activities in each program area to be effective means of day-to-day coordination. When staff members were asked what other program areas were doing with specific children, they usually replied that they hadn't had much time lately to talk to staff there or to visit the program area. No staff member reported using Goal Plan reports to obtain such information, even though Goal Plans from Children's Habilitation, for example, were detailed enough to obtain a good idea of the content of each intervention.

In theory, therapy aides on the unit staff, as primary therapists, were supposed to be responsible for ensuring coordination of the various program areas attended, according to interviews with the director of nursing services and with the deputy director for administration. In practice, these therapy aides appeared to have too little time and probably too little authority to obtain coordination effectively of such diverse program activities. When staff members mentioned occasions of conflicting treatment and were asked how they might handle it, their replies indicated they might mention it to the staff of the program area(s) involved, but if program staff did not change, normally nothing would be done. There seemed to be strong concern for respecting the assumed autonomy of each discipline, but little worry over the consequences for the effectiveness of treatment.

Underlying the different techniques used by staff in the separate program areas were basic differences in theoretical orientation between staff members regarding how much consistency of treatment procedures is desirable for the residents. Some felt that a variety of stimuli in terms of activities, diverse people, and changes in surroundings is best in order to encourage improvement in a variety of skills. If one activity or person doesn't "reach" the resident, something else is likely to. Other staff, particularly the behaviorally oriented psychologists, believed that these extremely retarded residents learn most rapidly by the highly structured, consistent associations among presentation of a stimulus, the client's response, and a rewarding consequence. The latter orientation is thus very compatible with the Goal Planning System. However, since little coordination of intervention content was occurring among the units and program areas, the "variety of stimuli" approach was being used by default.

Some efforts by individual staff to coordinate consistent follow-through on particular programs were viewed by other staff as attempts to dominate or to meddle in other departments' jurisdiction. One department head further noted that attempts to enforce consistency with Goal Planning would be professionally stifling to those in other disciplines. They would not have the chance to develop their own professional growth, if the approach of all disciplines had to be the same; thus, in his view, such consistency would not be satisfying to professional staff.

Overall, a major result of the lack of full implementation of Goal Planning was the absence of an effective means for obtaining continuity and coordination among the program areas providing interventions. Within limits of reasonable and humane treatment, each program area was nearly autonomous in planning its goals and methods. Such autonomy probably helped avoid overt conflict among the staff of the different departments, who had very different beliefs about appropriate treatment. But a price for this inter-staff harmony was probably paid in lower rates of learning, less motivation and/or more misbehaviors from the mentally retarded residents who were unable to protest if the demands made of them were contradictory.

ORGANIZATIONAL PROCESSES LEADING TO PARTIAL IMPLEMENTATION: MACRO-LEVEL COMPONENTS

The discussion of organizational processes developed in Chapter 2 detailed three levels of analysis for examining the context of program implementation: the macro level of the organization as a whole, the intermediate level of work-unit processes, and the micro level of individual cognitions and behavioral change. The results of the interview study at the Developmental Center, presented below, indicate that processes at all three levels were influential as sources of the variable degrees and problems of implementation of Goal Planning. While the variables analyzed at the intermediate and micro levels may seem to represent static characteristics, they are intended as indicators of the more dynamic processes which comprise the model. The use of interview data collected at one point in time prevents a more dynamic operationalization of these processes.

DECISION PROCESSES

At the macro level, processes surrounding the decision to adopt Goal Planning were examined in interviews with the senior administrators who were present at that time. Most reported that there was very little controversy over the initiation of Goal Planning; it is likely that there was little discussion of the assumptions underlying it as a treatment system. One staff member describes the events surrounding the adoption of Goal Planning as follows:

> [The chief psychologist] slid it in rather slow. It was started first on one unit and by [one program area] voluntarily. By evolution, it became *the* way of documenting treatment. But those disciplines not using it are not hurting [in terms of support from higher-level administrators].

The chief psychologist indicated that it was easily accepted by higher-level administrators when he came to the center in spring 1975 and was subsequently made official policy in a memo issued by the deputy director-clinincal. Yet, the extent to which Goal Planning had been incorporated into administrators' thinking about therapy is illustrated by noting that the official Policies and Procedures Manual for the center, prepared mostly in June 1976, included no mention of Goal Planning, although it did contain written guidelines for both "individual plan of care" and "clinical records."

The only resistance to the adoption of Goal Planning apparently focused on the additional paperwork it would require. Most administrators who were asked about the adoption of Goal Planning discussed it simply as a record-keeping system; some method of documentation was necessary to satisfy state and federal regulations, and Goal Planning was satisfactory for this purpose, although some would have preferred the medically developed Problem Oriented Record system. Those disciplines which did not use Goal Planning or had stopped using it objected particularly to the large volume of records which would be generated if they did several Goal Plans for each of the 15 to 20 residents seen daily by each staff member.

Other functions of Goal Planning, such as stimulating specific planning of treatment or facilitating coordination between disciplines and across shifts, seemed to have been largely ignored in the decision processes. There was little discussion of, among other matters, whether this orientation would be compatible with disciplines other than psychology; whether time, training, and supervision for this intensive written planning would be available to unit therapy aides; and whether Goal Planning would conflict with other types of state-mandated records. It was apparently thought to be a Psychology Department procedure that could be adopted without necessitating any changes in other organizational processes. Thus, the decision processes surrounding the adoption of the Goal Planning System did not resolve questions concerning its relationships with many other aspects of the center.

The lack of controversy over the adoption of Goal Planning seems related to the absence of staff members with a continuing interest, or "stake," in seeing the program implemented. Although the chief psychologist initiated the system and actively trained new employees in its use, he was not in a direct administrative line of supervision over any employees writing Goal Plans. Perhaps feeling incapable of influencing the dominant nursing hierarchy, the chief psychologist focused his later efforts on obtaining computerized processing of Goal Plans, another aspect of the system which was not operational at the center. The nursing staff, which did have direct supervisory responsibility over unit therapy aides, generally viewed Goal Planning as a Psychology Department responsibility. The psychology staff, who were in direct contact with therapy aides in an advisory role, expressed their interest in stimulating more unit-level therapy but felt that unit staff did not have the time and, sometimes, level of coordination to make a strong push for more Goal Planning worthwhile.

In summary, the initial decision to adopt Goal Planning was primarily done in compliance with the recommendations of the chief psychologist and to meet external regulations, rather than as a response to problems felt by the ultimate users, the unit and program staff. There were no staff with a strong interest in Goal Planning who had enough authority to push for fuller implementation.

CONTROL PROCESSES

As detailed above, there was apparently very little participation by the ultimate users in the decision to adopt Goal Planning. The decision process was centralized; yet, enforcement of the decision was decentralized. Each discipline was free to implement Goal Planning if it chose, with few sanctions or other consequences for not writing Goal Plans.

A mixture of centralized and decentralized control processes appeared to typify the operation of the center on most matters. Discipline heads emphasized favorably their nearly complete autonomy to run their own departments. Most departments were essentially democratic in their internal operations; some department heads and subordinates stressed professional autonomy for each staff member, while other departments had developed a team discussion approach for program planning and problem-solving. Yet, on matters of concern to the central administration—particularly having records meet inspection standards, enforcing safety standards, or avoiding unfavorable publicity—discipline heads did not have freedom to deviate from the regulations. Most staff, both supervisors and subordinates, seemed to accept these constraints as an inevitable part of working within a government agency.

However, the major personnel hierarchy—nursing services—which included all nurses and therapy aides assigned to residential units, was viewed as much more centralized, sometimes even arbitrarily authoritarian, by employees both inside and outside its jurisdiction. The director of nursing services spoke favorably of the "chain of command" style of organization control which is usual for nursing services in large hospitals, whereby policy directives move down the chain and problems or grievances also move up the chain until they are satisfactorily resolved. However, therapy aides complained that authority was too often used arbitrarily, particularly when changing their work assignment to another unit or shift. Since the background of the nursing supervisors emphasized physical well-being of the residents, therapy aides felt that their efforts toward therapy, and the residents' needs for therapy on the units, were not appreciated by the nursing hierarchy.

The hierarchical control system within nursing services also appeared to function in one direction only. Directives and decisions did move down the chain forcefully, but channels were blocked for messages moving up, particularly as they reached the nonnursing higher administrative levels. Several meetings were held for therapy aides and other staff to express their grievances and suggestions for change, but staff members believed these were ignored. Suggestions they believed to be practical went unheeded. Even several higher-level administrators criticized the lack of appropriate channels for expression of grievances, which became worse when the deputy director-clinical, previously the top of the hierarchy for therapeutic matters, resigned in fall 1977 and was not replaced. The frustration of therapy aides with the lack of higher-level support for adequate levels of staff and activities within the units broke into the public view when therapy aides obtained a sympathetic newspaper story on the front page of the local newspaper.

The consequences for Goal Planning of the control problems within nursing services were likely to be indirect. As further analyses at the intermediate level and individual levels will show, extent of Goal Planning was related both to unitwide routines and to individual employee satisfaction. With a control hierarchy which did not include Goal Planning within normally established routines, and with blocked hierarchical channels lowering morale, individual therapy aides were likely to have little motivation to exert extra effort toward developing Goal Plans.

The lack of coordinating processes among the various disciplines was mentioned by most discipline heads. As one program head explained,

> Lines of authority are very fuzzy here. Some heads of disciplines report to the Deputy Director-Clinical, some to the Chief of Service, but there's no clear distinction why. With our growing size, this is becoming more of a problem. There is no structure on top to resolve it, if there are conflicts between disciplines.

Although many discipline staff felt that interdisciplinary conflict was not much of a problem, few had examined carefully the consequences of diverse treatment programs encountered by individual residents, as detailed above. Thus, the consequences for Goal Planning of discipline-level autonomy were the lack of any detailed program coordination, plus the de facto acceptance of the "diversity of stimuli" philosophy of treatment.

OBTAINING RESOURCES

On the surface, it appeared that few additional resources would be needed to implement Goal Planning, since no technical equipment or specialized personnel are a part of the basic system. Yet, most staff interviewed saw it as more time-consuming, thus more staff-time intensive, if done well, than the more informal ad hoc therapeutic interactions it was meant to replace. Discipline staff not using Goal Planning cited particularly the extensive time required to write Goal Plans when instead they could be working with residents as a major objection to this system.

In the interviews, staff members were presented with a list of potential problems with Goal Planning and asked to rate each as a "major problem" in their work situation, a "minor problem," or "no problem at all." Of 12 problem statements, the highest problem rating (a mean of 2.5 out of a possible 3.0) was given to the statement, "Having enough staff on the unit to carry out the Goal Plan"—72 percent of the staff rated it a "major problem." The statement, "Not enough time to carry out Goal Plans after they are written" received the second-highest problem rating (a mean of 2.0 out of a possible 3.0), with 40 percent rating it a "major problem." As indicated above, the decision to adopt Goal Planning was apparently undertaken without much planning for the additional staff time it would require.

Furthermore, two new units were opened just before the interviews were conducted which required extensive reassignment of staff and training of new staff. This undoubtedly interrupted many ongoing Goal Plans, contributed to the low rate of follow-up with Milestones, and discouraged staff from initiating new Goal Plans. A high-level administrator acknowledged the staffing problems:

> With the opening of the new units, we just had sufficient staff for the resident's physiological needs, for food, clothing, and shelter. Next, we're trying to meet their programmatic needs by adding to the disciplines serving the new residents.

It is perhaps significant that in discussing staffing priorities for the expansion this administrator saw unit staff as providing for "physiological needs" and discipline staff as providing programs but failed to include unit-level therapy within his priorities for staff allocation. In summary, therapy aides were told they should be doing Goal-Planned therapy; extensive training for it was provided in their orientation period; but no additional unit staff was allocated to allow time to carry out Goal Plans on the units.

A lack of adequate resources for the full implementation of the Goal Planning system also was revealed in the unavailability of computerized processing for Goal Plans, in order to use them as a management information system. Although a significant part of the rationale for the system centers on the summarized information it can provide for administrators to review treatment programs, this use is severely limited when data from the Goal Plans have to be tabulated by hand. Although several such tabulations of data from Goal Plans had been done by the Psychology Department, the chief psychologist believed that these data were not being used by other department administrators. Interviews with ten senior administrators or heads of departments confirmed the psychologist's opinion, since none of them mentioned this summary data or a program review function when asked about Goal Planning. The lack of resources for a fundamental part of the system thus undermined its purposes and probably contributed to the feeling of many lower-level therapy aides that Goal Planning involved much useless paperwork.

RELATIONS WITH THE ENVIRONMENT

The organizational environment of a state mental health facility swarms with regulatory agencies. In addition to New York State Department of Mental Hygiene regulations, there were mandates from HEW's Developmental Disabilities Division which had to be followed in order for federal financing to be continued, as well as health and safety regulations, and relatively new guidelines for ensuring patients' civil rights. Further, for New York State facilities, a legal suit several years ago against the administration of Willowbrook Development Center resulted in a court degree (Willowbrook Consent Decree) specifying additional standards that were being applied statewide by the Department of Mental Hygiene. The struggle to keep up with regulations and pass various inspections was an obvious burden on higher-level administrators who bore the primary responsibility for fulfilling externally imposed standards.

One example of the likely influence of such regulations can be seen in the requirement for 5 and a half hours of "programs" per day for each resident, set by both the State Education Department and the quasi-regulatory Joint Commission on Accreditation of Hospitals. Since such treatment programs were usually provided off the residential units by the discipline staff, and inspection for compliance involved checking residents' daily schedules for their program time off-unit, unit staff also attempting to provide therapeutic interventions via Goal Planning were not counted toward meeting the external regulations. Thus, the allocation of staff, beyond those needed to provide for residents' physiological needs, to the program areas enabled increased resident time spent in programs and helped meet external standards, while assigning additional staff to units was apparently not recognized as therapeutic by external inspections.

In addition, the diverse regulations required that numerous types of records be kept. Other than the Goal Planning System, which met state and federal requirements for goal-oriented treatment records, there were complete medical records, monthly nursing notes, clothing inventories, vouchers for any expense for an individual resident, inspection and release forms before any outside visit by a resident (even to a parent's or relative's home), and semiannual evaluation reports from each program area for each resident. In addition, after any accident or parental complaint of suspected abuse (which were said to be frequently unfounded), there had to be an investigation and report signed by the chief of service. No wonder one administrator exclaimed, "We are frustrated and exhausted with paperwork!" Thus, regulations which are promulgated to prevent resident abuse and ensure high quality of care may have the consequence of consuming so much administrative time that little is left for internal coordination and support of staff.

Another impact of environmental pressures derived from the state-mandated procedures for quality review of medical records required senior staff from one developmental center to review the individual client records of another center, so that each center's records were reviewed by outsiders. Under this system, several senior staff spent considerable time reviewing another center's records. For example, the director of nursing services (whose jurisdiction encompassed all residential unit staff including nurses, therapy aides, and ward aides) reported that she spent three days each week for three months the previous year (approximately 15 percent of her total time that year) at another center investigating each client's records for deficiencies. This review reported 309 pages listing deficiencies in documentation among the more than 500 residents at that center. A similar review was done each year for each center. But, as one administrator pointed out, the focus of this review was mainly on the completeness of the records, not their quality, let alone the quality of the treatment actually delivered:

> You look for whether each program area's report is there, whether it was done within the required ten days after admission, not at the quality of the report. Even I do this when I'm on a review team. You have to, to get through all the records.

With this type of detailed record review pressuring the staff of each developmental center, but little review or use of Goal Plans, it is understandable that administrative staff's orientation was toward maintenance of the records even if Goal Plans did not get written and/or carried out.

This discussion of macro-level components has revealed a heavily constraining environment of regulatory agencies which preoccupied the attention of high-level administrators and thus helped to set priorities for lower-level staff. Allocation of staff resources appeared to be done in order to meet external standards, but the standards themselves were written in terms of resources spent rather than results achieved. Thus, there was little incentive for an administration under pressure to monitor the effects of its decision to adopt Goal Planning, nor even to push for implementation of the decision when such implementation was not effectively monitored. Administrators responsible for internal control processes responded with centralized rulings to enforce external standards, but allowed discipline-based autonomy in unregulated areas, such as the content and coordination of therapy provided. When an innovative program such as Goal Planning was introduced into this ongoing organizational system, it could be formally adopted to comply with external guidelines and internal professional interests. Yet, such adoption did not by itself generate sufficient changes in the internal organizational system to support actual implementation by individual staff members, as the following discussion of intermediate- and micro-level processes will reveal.

INTERMEDIATE-LEVEL PROCESSES

Data to examine intermediate- and micro-level processes were collected in the interviews with individual staff members, described in Chapter 3. Since the number of staff in comparable positions is large enough for quantitative analysis, variables measuring these processes were examined by multiple regression analysis. This statistical technique enables testing the explanatory influence of each of the independent variables in an equation while statistically holding constant the influence of the remaining independent variables. Thus, while the following discussion describes the construction and influence of each independent variable separately, the multiple regression analyses (in Tables 4.5 and 4.6) allow assessing that influence in the context of the whole set of variables.

Separate equations were estimated for the unit staff versus the program staff for several reasons. First, their overall level of Goal Plan writing differed considerably, with unit staff having written a mean of 1.6 plans each, while program area staff wrote a mean of 5.6 plans during the 14-month period coded. Second, their work situations were very different, because program staff engaged primarily in therapy oriented toward the discipline's label (such as Occupational Therapy, Special Education, and so forth) while Children's Habilitation was oriented toward behavioral psychology. In contrast, unit staff engaged in a variety of activities, including daily care, nursing care, supervision, and recreation with residents, as well as Goal-Planned therapy. Finally, because of their different work activities, several variables were available for the unit staff which were not asked of the program staff. The overall equations were therefore developed for the unit staff, then the same set of variables was applied to the program staff to examine their goodness of fit.

SUPERVISORY EXPECTATIONS

Therapy aides on the residential units were supervised and evaluated by nurses: a charge nurse was the head of each unit, while additional nurses supervised the evening shift. Even therapy aides with several years' experience or a higher educational level than many nurses were not given formal supervisory responsibility, although some might be given temporary responsibility if no nurse was available. Not surprisingly, when asked how they would describe their jobs, nurses tended to emphasize their nursing care and supervisory activities.

> My job is coordinator of health care for the children. . . . Sometimes babysitting, instead of nursing. . . . Seeing that the children receive proper medical attention and physical care. . . . Working with the therapy aides to make sure that assignments made are carried out.

Several nurses also emphasized an efficiency orientation in response to this open-ended question.

> There's a definite pattern here. We get a routine going so jobs are done quickly. . . . [Later, when discussing an individual detailed plan for teaching a child to feed himself] It would be better to have the whole unit on the same type of system, rather than individual techniques.

Consistent with behavioral principles and suggestions from previous literature (reviewed in Chapter 2), it was hypothesized that supervisory expectations toward therapy would encourage therapy aides to write Goal Plans.

In this study, such supervisory expectations were measured for unit therapy aides by several types of responses to a standard list of potential unit activities (question 11 on the interview schedule in Appendix A). Each unit staff member was asked to judge (on a scale of 4 to 1) the extent of his/her own time spent on each activity, the degree to which he/she felt each activity was a "central responsibility" of his/her job, and the perceived importance of each activity to his/her supervisor's expectations. In addition, the supervising nurses for each unit were asked to rate their expectations of activities for therapy aides as well as for themselves. From the list of 15 activities, five items relating to providing therapy were summed to form the Therapy Indexes, and five other items relating to daily care of residents were summed to form the Care Indexes. The range on each index is from 5 to 20, with higher scores indicating greater time, responsibility, or expectations for that type of activity.

These indexes for therapy and care from several perspectives thus allow a comparison of therapy aides' beliefs and perceptions of time spent with their perceptions of their supervisor's expectations and with the supervisor's own expectations. Mean scores for several indexes are listed in Table 4.3, along with their standard deviations. Comparing scores for therapy and care, these staff members saw themselves as spending more time on care than therapy (column a), but believed both were nearly equally important responsibilities (column b). Therapy aides believed their supervisors placed stronger expectations on care activities than therapy (see column c), but the supervising nurses themselves reported higher expectations for therapy than for care (column d). Thus, both therapy aides and nurses believed there should be stronger emphasis on therapy than the time presently devoted to it (indicated by column a), but this supervisory expectation was not perceived by therapy aides. These responses were also examined for each unit separately

TABLE 4.3
Mean Scores for Activity Indexes (Unit Staff Only)

		(a) Time spent	(b) Responsibility of own job	(c) Supervisor's expectations percieved	(d) Supervisor's expectations- actual
Therapy Indexes	Mean	11.34	14.38	12.67	15.85
	St. D.	(2.55)	(2.96)	(3.53)	(2.44)
Care Indexes	Mean	13.52	13.83	15.51	13.23
	St. D.	(2.57)	(2.74)	(2.43)	(2.92)
Number of Responses		65	65	49 (Therapy Aides only)	13 (RNs only)

(not shown here); the same pattern occurred in nearly every unit. The pattern of means shown in Table 4.3 thus indicates a gap in communication between therapy aides and nurses, particularly in the therapy aides' perception of nursing support for therapy.

The scores for supervisor's expectations for therapy as perceived by therapy aides, as well as the supervisor's actual expectation for therapy, were entered in the multiple regression analysis, with number of Goal Plans as the dependent variable. (The supervisor's actual expectation for therapy score for each unit and each shift was entered into the data set for those therapy aides. In order to fill in the missing data for nurses on perceived supervisory expectations, the mean of all therapy aides was used. This results in perceived supervisory expectations being a constant for the nurses, so the regression results for this variable apply only to therapy aides.) Descriptive information about each of the independent variables used in the final regression equations is provided in Table 4.4.

As the standardized regression coefficients for the unit staff in Table 4.5 indicate, both perceived and actual expectations are independently related to the number of Goal Plans written, although the influence of actual expectations is not strong enough to be statistically significant. That is, therapy aides tended to write more Goal Plans when they believed that their supervisor expected more therapy and when they worked on a unit and shift whose supervisor's actual expectations were higher. In addition, the zero-order correlation between perceived and actual supervisory expectations was $-.003$. Therapy aides' perceptions of their supervisor's support for therapy were not only lower than the nurses' expressed views, but there was no relationship between the strength of a supervisor's expectations for therapy and the therapy aide's view of the supervisor's expectations.

The situation facing many therapy aides was perhaps typified by the explanation of one senior-level nurse: "If therapy aides really want to do therapy, they could work it in" (among their other duties). Thus, therapy was viewed by this supervising nurse as an extra activity for strongly motivated employees, rather than a part of the day's normal activities. Other activities, such as giving baths, administering medications, or transporting residents to program areas, were not left to the therapy aides' individual motivations but were structured into the job routines. It is these differences in priorities, then, which were likely to be reflected in the therapy aides' perceptions of lower supervisory expectations for therapy than for care. But the positive regression coefficients reveal that supervisors' expectations—both actual and as perceived by therapy aides—did have an influence on therapy aides' tendency to write Goal Plans.

For the staff in program areas, no comparable activity indexes were available, since the activities in each area were too discipline-specific to compare on a standardized scale. Program staff were asked several items concerning their views of job responsibilities and agreement with supervisor, but these responses did not relate to their Goal Plan writing scores. Yet, interviews with each program area supervisor confirmed the proposition that when the supervisor firmly expected Goal Planning to be done, it became a part of the normal work

TABLE 4.4

Descriptive Information for Independent Variables, Unit Staff and Program Staff

Variables	Range	Reliability Coefficient	Unit Staff			Program Staff		
			Mean	St. Dev.	Number of Non-missing Responses	Mean	St. Dev.	Number of Non-missing Responses
Supervisor's Expectation for Therapy-Perceived by Therapy Aides	5-20	.73[a]	12.67	3.53	49			
Supervisor's Expectation for Therapy-Actual	5-20	.59[a]	15.85	2.44	13			
Presence of Routines	1-3	.90[b]	2.48	.69	65	2.47	.90	19
Time on Unit (in Months)	1-38	—	12.46	9.69	65	13.92	8.65	24
Discussion with Co-workers-Frequency	1-3	.70[b]	2.61	.61	49	2.45	.51	22
Age	18-58	—	31.18	10.35	65	27.21	5.95	24
Satisfaction with Job	1-5	—	3.71	1.07	65	4.38	.71	24
"Professional" Reading	1-3	.73[b]	2.06	.56	64	2.46	.59	24
Attitude Toward Goal Plans	1-4	.73[b]	2.36	.98	64	2.48	1.33	21
Liking for Therapy	0-5	—	1.68	1.24	60			

[a] Reliability coefficient for this index is coefficient alpha (Nunally, 1967), a measure of internal consistency.
[b] Reliability coefficient for this score is the percentage of agreement between two coders.

TABLE 4.5
Regression Coefficients for Number of Goal
Plans from Given Predictor Variables

Predictor Variables	Unit Staff (N = 65)		Program Staff (N = 24)	
	b	Standardized betas	b	Standardized betas
Intermediate-Level Variables				
Supervisory Expectations:				
Perceived	.17	.22*		
Actual	.17	.16		
Presence of Routines	.48	.14	6.21	.62***
Time on Unit, In Months	.09	.37***	.41	.45***
Discussions with Co-workers-				
Frequency	-1.40	-.31***	-2.66	-.16
Micro-Level—Individual Variables				
Age	-.08	-.35***	.30	.22
Satisfaction with Job	.53	.24*	2.04	.18
"Professional" Reading	1.20	.28**	2.10	.15
Attitude Toward Goal Plans	.41	.17	1.95	.30
Liking for Therapy	.54	.27**		
(Constant)	-5.69		-36.08	
R^2		.40		.60
F		3.58***		3.48**
df		10/54		7/16

*$p<.10$ **$p<.05$ ***$p<.01$

expectations held by that program area staff, and more Goal Planning was actually accomplished. For example, the head of Children's Habilitation held a doctorate in school psychology and reported a strongly behavioral emphasis in her graduate training. This program was also structured by a set schedule of one-to-one therapy hours, and Goal Plans for each client were expected and reviewed by the supervisor. As the total of 121 Goal Plans prepared by the CH staff indicates, this program had firmly integrated Goal Planning into its daily operations. By comparison, the heads of Physical Therapy and Occupational Therapy had strong client-centered orientations, but did not incorporate the behavioral emphasis on structured consistency of therapy in their approach. To these supervisors, Goal Planning involved too much unnecessary paperwork; therefore, they did not require it of their staff. Even though the work structure of one-to-one therapy sessions within these disciplines would be compatible with individual behavioral goals, the absence of strong supervisor support for it undoubtedly contributed to the fact that staff in these disciplines had written no Goal Plans at all.

STANDARD OPERATING ROUTINES

The differences in supervisory expectations among the various program areas were closely related to the different operating procedures of these departments. A structure of one-to-one therapy sessions, scheduled times for specific activities, and detailed data records of each client response, as the work situation was structured in Children's Habilitation, provided a set of work routines compatible with Goal Planning. By contrast, disciplines that worked with groups of residents, such as Special Education and Vocational Rehabilitation, tended to have a variety of activities occurring at the same time, with multiple informal objectives and less structured interaction between staff members and residents. These work procedures were less compatible with Goal Planning. The Special Education teachers had stopped using this sytem by fall 1977, even though they had written numerous plans the previous school year. In Vocational Rehabilitation, individual Goal Plans were prepared primarily for handling residents' misbehaviors, while a detailed token-economy system provided structured incentives for the standard routine of simulated work activities.

Within the residential units, Goal-Planned therapy as one aspect of a therapy aide's work role had been, in essence, added to a more traditional role for such mental health workers that emphasized efficient care of residents. The major routines were oriented toward the daily care of residents, although the extent to which structured routines regulated work activities varied considerably, particularly depending on the frequency of residents' tendency to have "outbursts" of behavioral problems requiring immediate physical restraint. However, each unit did have a daily work schedule of therapy aides' assignments, for example, to take residents to their programs or to other appointments, and for giving baths or giving medication. Yet, since Goal-Planned therapy procedures were considered by nurses an individual responsibility rather than a part of necessary unit routines, carrying out the plans was usually not built into the daily work schedules drawn up by the supervising nurse.

Consequently, the unit staff had difficulty obtaining consistency among the various shifts to carry out plans. In response to the standard list of potential problems with Goal Planning presented in the interviews, 61 percent of the unit staff rated "Getting other staff on the unit to carry out the Goal Plan" as either a major or a minor problem. Although one unit had recently set up a bulletin board to attempt to increase consistency of follow-through on Goal Plans, most units had not yet integrated it into their ongoing routines.

In addition, the staff shortages and nursing efficiency orientation of some supervisors tended to encourage establishing routines that saved time, rather than those which might increase residents' skills. "Not enough time" was a constant refrain in therapy aides' discussion of Goal Planning:

> If a therapy aide takes 20 minutes to let Stacy walk to her program [instead of pushing her in a wheelchair], these other kids may not get to their programs at all!

Particularly in those units whose residents required extensive help in eating, dressing, and other self-care skills, teaching the resident to do these skills required much more staff time in the short run than simply doing the task for them. Efficient operating procedures, in this case, were not likely to be the most effective for teaching new skills via Goal Planning.

A question measuring the extent of predictable work routines was included in the interviews by asking, "Do you know fairly well when you come into work what you will be doing that day?" Responses to this open-ended question were coded on a three-value scale ranging from 3 for those who said the work tends to be predictable to 1 for those who said there was much change from day to day. Descriptive statistics for this and other independent variables are provided in Table 4.4. The few missing-data cases for this variable, the presence of routines, within the program staff were filled in by the mean for the remaining program staff.

Another variable thought to relate to the predictability of routines for individual staff members is the length of time working on that particular unit, in months. This "time on unit" variable is likely to reflect the staff member's familiarity with that unit, its procedures and residents, as well as his/her length of service in the center as a whole. With such knowledge of unit routines, the therapy aide was better able to write a Goal Plan that could be carried out within the situation on that unit. A frequent complaint of therapy aides was that they were switched arbitrarily from one unit to another by the nurse administrators, particularly when new units were opened. The data comparing time on job (total number of months employed at the center) with time on unit revealed that 68 percent of the unit staff had been employed at the center for one year or more, but about a third of these members had been assigned to their present unit less than a year. Together with new staff just hired within one year, fully 55 percent of the unit staff had been on the same unit for less than one year.

Both the presence of routines and length of time on unit relate positively to the number of Goal Plans written by individual staff members, among both unit and program area staff. The standardized regression coefficients shown in Table 4.5 show a positive, but not quite statistically significant, association of routines with Goal Plans among the unit staff (.14), but a very strong association of the same variables (.62) among the program staff. Time on unit is strongly and significantly related to Goal Planning among both the unit staff (.37) and the program staff (.45). Staff who said there was a predictable routine in their work location tended to write more Goal Plans. Similarly, the longer the time worked on a particular unit, the more plans a staff member wrote. If total time on job is also entered into the regression equation (shown in Table 4.6), the influence of time on unit is decreased somewhat (from a standardized regression coefficient of .37 to .23) with time on job showing a coefficient of .24. Thus, the effect on Goal Planning of time on unit is partly due to greater length of experience at the center, but also related to one's specific experience in the particular unit. It is likely that the longer time on a unit allowed knowledge of the unit's residents and operating procedures to develop, which in turn might have stimulated Goal Planning for relevant treatment procedures.

TECHNICAL REQUIREMENTS OF THE INNOVATION

The review of previous literature in Chapter 2 discussed the likely differential effectiveness of various methods of presenting a new program, depending on its technical requirements. While an innovation whose technical details are fully specified in advance might be adequately introduced by information transmittal alone, such as with a written manual, an innovation requiring details to be created by the user or involving role changes within an ongoing work group is likely to need active participatory learning on a continuing basis in order to solve implementation problems as they arise.

Obviously, this investigation of the introduction of Goal Planning to the Developmental Center did not allow examination of differences in technical requirements, since these were a constant for all users. Yet, the fact that Goal Planning did require numerous details to be developed by the users—the choice of appropriate goals for each resident, the specification of therapeutic procedures to work toward the goals, and the development of communication links among various staff needed to carry out a plan—suggests that technical development problems might have been anticipated.

TABLE 4.6
Standardized Regression Coefficients for Number of Goal Plans Showing Additional Possible Predictors—Unit Staff Only
(N = 65)

Predictor Variables							Equations							
	(1)	(2)	(3)	(4)	(5)	(6)	(7)	(8)	(9)	(10)	(11)	(12)	(13)	(14)
Intermediate—Level Variables														
Supervisory Expectations-Perceived	.20	.22	.18	.18	.18	.21	.22	.22	.22	.22	.21	.21	.20	.20
Supervisory Expectations-Actual	.16	.15	.15	.12	.14	.15	.16	.16	.15	.15	.16	.16	.15	.17
Presence of Routines	.17	.14	.16	.16	.19	.14	.14	.14	.13	.14	.13	.14	.16	.21
Time on Unit, in Months	.23	.37	.36	.33	.39	.38	.37	.37	.36	.37	.36	.37	.37	.37
Discussions with Co-workers	-.32	-.31	-.34	-.36	-.33	-.31	-.31	-.31	-.32	-.31	-.32	-.31	-.32	-.32
Micro-Level Variables														
Age	-.39	-.36	-.33	-.36	-.36	-.34	-.35	-.35	-.35	-.34	-.35	-.35	-.36	-.27
Satisfaction with Job	.26	.23	.23	.27	.23	.19	.24	.24	.26	.24	.25	.24	.22	.30
"Professional" Reading	.31	.28	.27	.25	.30	.29	.28	.28	.29	.28	.27	.28	.27	.23
Liking for Therapy	.27	.26	.26	.26	.28	.27	.27	.27	.26	.25	.27	.27	.28	.25
Attitude toward Goal Plans	.16	.17	.16	.17	.16	.20	.17	.17	.17	.17	.15	.17	.17	.25

TABLE 4.6 (Continued)

Predictor Variables	Equations													
	(1)	(2)	(3)	(4)	(5)	(6)	(7)	(8)	(9)	(10)	(11)	(12)	(13)	(14)
Additional Variables														
Time on Job	.24													
Hours of Training		-.03												
Contact with Psychologists-Frequency			.10											
Communication Frequency Index				.16										
Reaction of Co-workers to Goal Planning					.15									
Differences of Opinion Among Co-workers						-.17								
Level of Education							.01							
Number of Psychology Courses								-.01						
Job Descriptive Indexes														
Work									-.05					
Pay										-.05				
Promotions											-.05			
Supervisor												.01		
Co-workers													.09	
Belief in Goal Planning														.30
R^2	.43	.40	.41	.42	.41	.42	.40	.40	.40	.40	.40	.40	.41	.44
F	3.58	3.21	3.05	3.19	3.39	3.35	3.20	3.20	3.21	3.22	3.22	3.14	3.29	4.20
df	11/53	11/53	11/53	11/49	11/53	11/50	11/53	11/53	11/53	11/53	11/53	11/53	11/53	10/54

Training on the technical procedures for Goal Planning was included in the six-week orientation and training program for all new unit staff. All but four of the 65 unit staff reported at least some training sessions for Goal Planning. However, only 13 of the 24 program staff stated they received this training, which was oriented particularly toward the residential units. The training sessions for Goal Planning normally occurred within the new therapy aide's first three months on the job; there were no continuing problem-solving sessions on a regular, formal basis. Further, the extensiveness of training for Goal Planning, in terms of number of hours, varied considerably among the groups of therapy aides which began work at different times.

Staff members interviewed were asked to estimate the number of hours of training for Goal Planning they had received. Responses ranged from zero to 48 hours, with a mean of 13 hours estimated by the unit staff and 8.5 hours by the program staff. Since many respondents stated they could not remember how many hours their sessions on Goal Planning had been, these perceptions are likely to be, at best, rough estimates. It is not surprising, then, that perceived number of hours of training was not a substantial predictor of Goal Plan writing for the unit staff. If number of training hours is included in the set of predictor variables, as shown in Table 4.6, the standardized regression coefficient is $-.03$ for the unit staff, thus contributing no predictability to this equation. For program staff, the comparable coefficient is .13, thus showing slight, but not significant, association.

Further, scores on two other measures for the unit staff support the proposition that initial, factual training is inadequate for an innovation whose technical requirements demand creativity and role relearning from the users. Staff were asked to rate the extent of difficulty presented by 12 aspects of Goal Planning that might be considered problem areas, such as "not enough time to write Goal Plans," "knowing what is a good therapeutic intervention," and "obtaining coordination among staff." Both a total problem score and four problem indexes relating to specific types of problems showed *positive* relationships with number of Goal Plans written (a correlation coefficient of .23 for total problem scores with number of Goal Plans). Staff who had written more plans felt there were more problems in the system. Similarly, staff members were asked how clear was their understanding of Goal Planning after the initial training. Those who had written *more* plans reported they felt *less* clear about how to do it (the correlation coefficient here was −.33). Since these relationships are negative, they were not entered in the final regression analysis. The causal direction of influence was likely to be from writing more Goal Plans to perceiving more problems and feeling less clear about the system, rather than in the other direction. Some comments by the therapy aides when discussing the adequacy of the training illustrate this interpretation: "The best teacher is actually doing it." "There's always something new to learn." "At first, I just knew how to fill out the forms. You have to develop the techniques to use in the actual Plan."

These findings indicate that the type and timing of training provided was inadequate for overcoming the problems posed by the technical requirements of the Goal Planning system. While the formal procedures for writing a Goal Plan involved simply filling in the spaces correctly on a printed form, which those who had done little actual Goal Planning thought they understood, in reality the development of appropriate techniques to include in a plan was more complex and was recognized as more problematic by staff with more experience using it. The desirability of continued problem-solving sessions for the implementation of Goal Planning was shown by these findings. In fact, when asked to comment on the adequacy of the training sessions, 20 staff members (38 percent of the 52 who commented on the content of the training) replied that greater focus was needed on techniques for reaching the goals identified. Thus, the training provided for the implementation of this innovation was not congruent with its technical requirements.

COMMUNICATION FLOW

The preceding discussion of a need for problem-solving sessions on Goal Planning, as well as the literature reviewed in

Chapter 2, have emphasized the importance of open communications to facilitate use of a new program, particularly communication with the source of the innovation. At the Developmental Center, the researcher expected that the frequency of contact with psychologists would increase Goal Planning, since this system is based on principles of psychology and was introduced by the chief psychologist. This hypothesized relationship was *not* strongly supported by the interview data.

The regression coefficient for frequency of contact with psychologists (on a scale of 6 for "once a day or more" to 1 for "never") was .10 among the unit staff, as shown in Table 4.6. That Goal Plan writing was not more strongly related to frequency of contact with psychologists was an unexpected outcome. One explanation for the lack of relationship is that the level of contact with psychologists was generally high; 52 percent of the unit staff reported discussions with a psychologist at least several times per week. Although frequency of contact differed somewhat among the units and between shifts, a generally high level of contact did not differentially relate to those writing Goal Plans and thus did not show a strong statistical relationship.

Additional data on the activities of psychologists was collected by asking each psychologist to keep a brief record of his/her location and activity for each half-hour segment over a two-week period. Tabulation of these records supported the fact that psychologists were in frequent contact with the unit staff: An average of 23 percent of their time was spent on the units, with an additional 19 percent spent in meetings—mostly resident staffings or working with undergraduate students on a unit-based project. Thus, the psychologists seemed to have developed a pattern of frequent and informal contact with the unit staff that might have allowed them to give informal support and supervision to therapy aides attempting Goal Planning. Yet, little information was available on the content of these informal contacts, for example, to indicate whether psychologists emphasized Goal Planning as a valuable tool for planning and/or communication or supported the feeling of some therapy aides that writing plans was mostly just more paperwork.

Another measure of communication flow was an index of perceived communication frequency for unit staff with all program staff. This was constructed from interview items which asked the respondant to rate on a scale of 1 for "never" to 6 for "once a day or more" how often he/she discussed client-related problems with any staff members in each of the programs. The responses for six program areas, plus "social workers" and "psychologists," were summed, then divided by the number of programs rated, to yield an index of communication frequency. While the overall mean of 2.74 for this index (standard deviation of .75) indicates a level of contact averaging about once a month for each program area, there was some variation among the units studied.

When this communication index was entered into the regression equation (see Table 4.6), the resulting standardized coefficient of .16 for the unit staff indicated a positive, but not statistically significant, relationship with number of Goal Plans written. That is, individual unit staff who reported more frequent resident-oriented communications with program staff had a slight tendency to write more Goal Plans. Yet, the strength of the relationship was not high; this index was not available for enough program area staff to enter it into their equation; and the direction of influence was ambiguous. Therefore, the communication index was not included in final "best fit" equations whose coefficients are listed in Table 4.5.

The importance of open and detailed communication among the staff in various programs working with the same residents should not be dismissed. As detailed by the earlier discussion of the consequences of the intermittent implementation of Goal Planning, the programs for individual residents may be contradictory if little interchange on goals and techniques take place. That these problems were recognized by some unit staff is shown by the following comments:

Some of the Goal Plans on the unit don't agree with what is done in the workshop. This may cause outbursts by the residents, because there is not a thorough understanding of the Goal Plan by all staff.

Some [program staff] never consult us, and our staff is frustrated. For example, [a program staff member] said she would come to the unit to show our staff how to teach self-feeding. But the tray had to be ordered early, then was sent back nearly full. The child didn't eat! How can that be teaching self feeding?

In this case, the rationale behind the program staff's method was not communicated clearly to the unit staff, so nearly six months of efforts to stimulate self-feeding on this unit were not followed up regularly by unit staff and self-feeding skills deteriorated. Thus, the rather limited flow of verbal communication among the separate disciplines reflected the lack of a mechanism for overall program coordination. Although the psychologists had fairly frequent contact with most unit staff members, they did not have the authority to require coordination among all the disciplines. Increased Goal Planning and more frequent communications with program staff were slightly linked, as shown by their regression coefficient, but the weakness of this link may reflect the lack of emphasis at the macro level on program coordination among the disciplines.

WORK GROUP NORMS

Organizational literature suggests that the immediate work group dynamic of acceptance or rejection of an innovation can be a powerful determinant of its implementation. This potential influence was also recognized by some staff at the center. When asked his view of the present degree of success of Goal Planning, one social worker explained:

A lot of Plans are not carried out. New staff are trained in it, and told they have a quota of at least three Goal Plans during their first year. They may be enthusiastic and try it, but there is peer pressure of other staff. Often, this works against carrying out a Plan if older therapy aides [having more job seniority] think it is a waste of time. So, functionally the plans don't get carried out and it's not really a help then to require new therapy aides to write them.

Several questions were included in the interviews to attempt to uncover work group norms with quantitative indicators. For example, staff were asked what reactions they had received from co-workers in their efforts at Goal Planning. The results showed generally positive views of co-worker support—among unit staff, only 16 percent reported that co-workers were neutral or negative in their reaction to Goal Planning. Probably because of the low variability of this measure, the reaction of co-workers did not contribute substantially to predicting Goal Planning (the standardized regression coefficient with number of Goal Plans, for the unit staff, was .15). How much this measure reflected real group norms of support for Goal Planning versus the staff member's desire to project an image of a cohesive peer group is impossible to determine from the data collected.

However, another measure less directly tied to Goal Planning in the interviews shows somewhat different results. An open-ended question asked about the nature and frequency of discussions with co-workers concerning problems of their work. Responses about frequency were coded from 1 for "less than once a week" to 3 for "every day." (Missing data on this measure, mostly for nurses who were not asked this question, were filled in with the mean score for the respondent's unit, in order to reflect the group norm as much as possible.) This variable was strongly predictive of Goal Planning, but in a negative direction. The standardized regression coefficients shown in Table 4.5 are -.31 for the unit staff and -.16 for program staff. That is, the more frequently a therapy aide discussed things with co-workers, the fewer Goal Plans he/she wrote. Further, the more differences of opinion among his/her co-workers reported by a therapy aide, which probably reflected less cohesiveness on the unit, the fewer Goal Plans written (see equation 6 in Table 4.6). The pattern of these findings suggests that those who discussed unit activities frequently with their co-workers did not perceive in these discussions much pressure toward Goal Planning; those who did write more Goal Plans may have tended to be "lone wolves," not strongly integrated into a cohesive work group. Thus, the group norms in this situation appeared to be depressing the level of Goal Plan writing, either by expressions of skepticism concerning the value of this system or, in at least one strongly therapeutically oriented unit, by facilitating within-unit coordination of therapy without using many written Goal Plans.

SUMMARY

Several intermediate-level variables have been shown to be predictive of the number of Goal Plans written by individual staff members. These are summarized by the regression coefficients shown in Table 4.5. Supervisory expectations for therapy—both perceived and actual—the presence of routines, longer time working in the specific unit, and fewer discussions with co-workers all had fairly strong influences on writing Goal Plans for the unit staff. For the program staff, those variables at this level which were available quantitatively also showed similar relationships with Goal Planning, with the influence of "routines" being much stronger for the program staff than for the unit staff. One hypothesized relationship which was not supported strongly by these data was the influence of communication flow. Neither the frequency of contact with psychologists nor an index of communication with program staff showed significant regression coefficients, although both were in the expected direction. Finally, an analysis of the type of training provided, in relationship to the technical requirements of this innovation, revealed no influence on Goal Planning by more hours of initial training but continuing high problem ratings and lack of clarity associated with writing more Goal Plans.

The components at this level of the model have thus shown substantial influence for these processes of the work setting in explaining individual staff behaviors. Further discussion of the predictive power of this part of the model will be deferred until after the individual-level variables have been described, for both intermediate- and micro-level components showed strong influences on Goal Planning.

INDIVIDUAL-LEVEL VARIABLES

The model developed in Chapter 2 describes three types of individual variables which are likely to generate individual differences in the degree of implementing a new program: behavioral skills sufficient for the innovation's technical requirements, incentives for changed performance, and cognitive supports of compatible beliefs and attitudes. These might be summarized by viewing individual implementation as a process of role change, which, for unit staff doing Goal Planning, involved integrating therapeutic activities into a nursing-oriented role structure emphasizing efficient routines along with humane care. Yet, the administrative assumption officially in force at the Developmental Center was that Goal Planning was an individual responsibility, rather than an activity mutually supported by each unit's group of staff. Therefore, it might be expected that individual-level variables would have particularly strong effects.

BEHAVIORAL SKILLS

The possession of appropriate technical skills, or the capacity to develop them, was hypothesized to be an important component of implementation at the individual level. In addition to the amount of training specifically focused on the new program, this component would include demographic variables such as age or education, or more specific educational experiences relating directly to the new program.

As discussed above, the reported number of hours of training for Goal Planning was not related to the number of plans written. Further, neither the level of education nor the number of college-level psychology courses taken was a predictor of Goal Planning. Level of education was coded on a scale of 1 for less than high school graduation to 7 for possession of a graduate degree. The extent of higher education was actually rather high for this type of job: 63 percent of the unit staff and 83 percent of the program staff had at least some college, while 20 percent of the unit staff and 75 percent of the program staff were college graduates. Yet, the standardized regression coefficients for education for predicting number of Goal Plans were only .01 for the unit staff and a negative, -.18, for the program staff.

In order to look for an influence of educational experiences that might be directly relevant to Goal Planning, the number of psychology courses the respondent had taken was also examined. The regression coefficients for this variable with number of Goal Plans were -.01 for unit staff and .06 for the program staff. Again, a fairly high level of achievement in psychology was exhibited: 29 percent of the unit staff and 71 percent of the program staff reported they had taken four or more college-level psychology courses, while only 28 percent of the unit staff and none of the program staff had not taken any psychology courses.

The only individual background variable which was related to Goal Planning was the staff member's age, and this worked in opposite directions. For the unit staff, the standardized regression coefficient of -.35 means that younger staff tended to write more Goal Plans, while the coefficient for the program staff of .22 indicates that older staff wrote more. The coefficient for the program staff, who number only 24, may have been heavily influenced by one older staff member who happened to work in Children's Habilitation and therefore wrote many Goal Plans. But it is not clear from the data why younger staff in the units wrote more plans, since this contradicts the hypothesis that older staff would have acquired more behavioral skills. Further, the regression analysis should have controlled for the influence of variables such as professional orientation, liking for therapy, or a favorable attitude toward Goal Planning (to be discussed below) which might differentiate older and younger staff.

The lack of influence for education and number of psychology courses was also puzzling. Some clues for interpretation may be provided by examining correlation coefficients with other variables. Among unit staff, level of education was negatively related to perceived supervisor's expectation for therapy (correlation coefficient of -.22), negatively related to overall job satisfaction (r of -.26), but positively related to a measure of role conflict (r of .33). Similar correlations were shown by these variables with the number of psychology courses taken. Those with higher levels of education tended to perceive more role conflict, less satisfaction, and less supervisory support for therapy; all these variables would tend to counteract any increased behavioral skill the therapy aide had acquired through education.

Perhaps such depressors of motivation for extra efforts toward therapy derived from staff's frustrated hopes for better jobs from their investment in education. But a similar depression of internally based motivations might occur from macro-level organizational components such as the lack of functioning vertical communication channels, the scarcity of staff time to carry out Goal Plans on the units, and the ambiguity of supervisory support for Goal Planning. Some comments made by therapy aides when asked about their overall job satisfaction illustrate this interpretation:

> We are expected to be super human, especially when they open new units without sufficient numbers of staff. It's not fair for the residents when staff don't have enough time.

> The pressures are intense. There are three-way battles between ourselves, some program areas, and the administration. . . . We're not given credit for our ideas [by the higher administration] and this brings the level of satisfaction down.

However, others mentioned the lack of promotion possibilities, or perception of unfair promotions ("based on friendship"). Thus, both interpretations may be influential for the failure of advanced technical skills to have increased the implementation of this program.

INCENTIVES

As the preceding discussion has suggested, the presence of appropriate behavioral skills may not be adequate to stimulate changed behavior, if no incentives for changed performance are present. Such incentives might be either externally provided rewards, such as increased pay or possibility for promotion, or internal satisfactions from seeing progress in clients or using one's professional skills. Examination of the structure of potential incentives is especially important when, as with the introduction of Goal Planning, the innovation was not built into the daily routines but was considered an individual responsibility to be "worked into" the unit's schedule of tasks. However, since Developmental Center workers were civil service employees, neither level of pay nor likelihood of promotion (for therapy aides) was available as an incentive for individual performance.

A number of variables were examined as potential indicators of internally provided incentives for increased Goal Planning. For example, each respondent completed the job satisfaction scales designed by Smith, Kendall, and Hulin (1969), called the Job Descriptive Index, which contains separate measures of satisfaction with the work itself, pay, promotions, the supervisor, and co-workers. Although such satisfactions might function as internal motivations for increased Goal Planning, none of these measures showed substantial regression coefficients with the number of Goal Plans written.

Further, it had been anticipated that the index of problems with Goal Planning, previously described in the section on technical requirements, would provide a measure of the perceived "costs" of doing Goal Planning and thus would be a measure of personal disincentives. However, the relationship was found to be positive rather than negative: Those who wrote more Goal Plans also felt there were more problems in the system. Therefore, this variable cannot be considered a direct indicator of a motivation to do Goal Planning. Although the higher problem scores received by those who had written some plans may in fact depress their motivation to write additional plans, the data collected at one point for this study were not sufficient to examine this more complex causal process.

Nevertheless, several other measures of incentives did show strong positive relationships with Goal Planning. One item asked the respondent to rate his/her overall level of job satisfaction from "very satisfied" (coded as 5) to "very dissatisfied" (coded as 1). This measure of job satisfaction had a standardized regression coefficient with Goal Planning of .24 for the unit staff and .18 for the program staff (see Table 4.5). Since the general level of satisfaction was high (62 percent of unit staff and 88 percent of program staff replied they were "fairly satisfied" or "very satisfied"), it is likely that the association with Goal Planning was because those who were less satisfied consequently felt less motivated to do Goal Planning. Several comments about this question quoted earlier revealed a felt lack of appreciation for therapy aides' extra efforts toward planning therapy; thus, this satisfaction measure may also be an indicator of a lack of externally based social rewards of praise or approval from those with higher status in this organizational system.

Finally, a measure of the "professional orientation" that has been found to be associated with willingness to innovate was obtained here by a question asking the extent to which the staff member ever read outside materials related to mental retardation. Responses to this open-ended question were coded on a three-value scale of 1 for no, 2 for infrequently (less than once a month), and 3 for any frequency over once a month. The overall level of this outside reading was not astoundingly high; about 20 percent of the unit staff and 42 percent of the program staff reported they read something relating to their jobs at least once a month. But the standardized regression coefficients with Goal Planning of .28 for the unit staff and .15 for the program staff showed the positive influence of such professionalism. Those who did outside reading also may have obtained internal satisfaction from attempts to translate their reading into active therapy via Goal Planning. That more frequent reading was not simply a result of higher educational level was indicated by correlation coefficients between education and "professional reading" of only .16 for the unit staff and .03 for the program staff.

In summary, several variables which were likely to be indicators of internally felt incentives were found to be positively related to Goal Planning—specifically, overall job satisfaction and "professional" reading. However, other expected outcomes relating to incentives, particularly a smaller score on the problem index and higher satisfaction on the specific Job Descriptive Index scores, were not substantiated by the regression analyses.

COGNITIVE SUPPORTS

The final individual-level component to be considered is the structure of individual cognitions about the innovation. The major hypothesis here is that if staff members like the new program and believe it will accomplish its purpose, these cognitive supports will encourage implementation by avoiding stressful cognitive dissonance between beliefs and actions.

These ideas were supported by several variables in this study. One such variable was a "liking for therapy" index, formed by counting the number of therapy activities within the activity list which a respondent chose in response to the question, "Are there any of these activities that you like a lot and want to do more often?" (This was the same activity list used to form the supervisory expectations indexes.) Since there were five therapy activities, scores for this index could range from zero to five activities. The actual mean score for the unit staff was 1.7, or an average of just under two therapy activities chosen. This index had a standardized regression coefficient of .27 with number of Goal Plans for the unit staff. It was not available for the program staff because the activities list was not applicable to their situation.

Two indicators of subjective orientation toward Goal Planning also showed positive predictive relationships. One was a score for overall attitude toward Goal Planning coded from responses to the open-ended question, "What do you think of Goal Planning, in general?" Responses were coded on a four-value scale of 1 for predominantly negative to 4 for predominantly positive comments, with the two values in between applied to mixed positive and negative responses. This attitude indicator showed not quite statistically significant standardized regression coefficients with number of Goal Plans written of .17 for the unit staff and .30 for the program staff.

Another, more specific question concerned belief in the efficacy of Goal Plans to actually change residents' behaviors or skills (coded on a scale of 1 to 3: "no change likely for most of our residents" to "most Goal Plans do help change behaviors").

If included in the regression equation for unit staff in place of "attitude toward Goal Plans," the standardized regression coefficient for belief in Goal Plans was .30 (see Table 4.6), indicating a fairly substantial positive influence. Unfortunately, this measure was available for only 51 of the 65 unit staff and 10 of the 24 program staff. (It was not on the written questionnaire, but was intended to be asked as a follow-up question. However, one interviewer had particularly large numbers of missing responses and had probably forgotten to ask it of many staff members.) Because of the large amount of missing data, this variable was not included in the final regression analysis of Table 4.5. Yet, "belief in Goal Planning" was highly interrelated with the overall "attitude toward Goal Planning" measure, as shown by a correlation coefficient of .59. Therefore, the "attitude" score was likely to reflect the respondent's beliefs about the efficacy of Goal Planning, but less directly; hence the lower regression coefficient for "attitude toward Goal Planning" than for "beliefs."

In summary, the cognitive support variables of liking therapy activities and positive attitude or belief did influence Goal Planning behavior, even when other individual and organizational components were controlled in regression analyses. In a work situation that was ambivalent concerning Goal Planning, with formal requirements for it present but its incorporation into work routines largely absent and supervisor expectations ambiguous, individual cognitions and internally based incentives did have independent influence on the day-to-day implementation of this program.

CONCLUSIONS:
UTILITY OF THE MODEL

The data on Goal Planning examined by means of the regression analyses in Table 4.5 revealed a reasonably high explanatory power for the analytical model proposed. The R^2 coefficients, which show percentage of variance explained by these equations, were .40 for the unit staff and .60 for the program staff. For the program staff, the small number of respondents prevented many of the individual regression coefficients from reaching statistical significance, but their values were large enough to confirm processes very similar to those affecting the unit staff. The large coefficients for variables indicating use of standard operating procedures, the presence of routines, and time on unit substantiate the overriding influence of differential work routines among the program areas. But the fact that the overall explanatory power of the equation is .60 even among the program staff, when the indicators for the concepts in the model were developed in relation to the unit staff, helps confirm the overall conceptual validity of the model.

Among the unit staff, most of the components conceptualized at the intermediate and micro levels did contribute to the explanation of individual implementation of Goal Planning. At the intermediate level, supervisory expectations, both as expressed by unit supervisors and as perceived by unit workers; the presence of unit routines and longer time working within the unit; and work group norms, as measured by the frequency of discussions with co-workers, all contributed to explaining number of Goal Plans written, although the influence of work group norms was negative. Only the indicators of communication flow did not show strong relationships with the dependent variable, Goal Planning, but the direction of their weak influence was positive. At the individual level, measures thought to indicate greater behavioral skills, such as level of education, number of psychology courses, and hours of training for Goal Planning, surprisingly were not influential here; the only individual background variable having explanatory power was the strong negative effect of age. However, individual variables relating to internal incentives, such as job satisfaction and "professional" reading, as well as cognitive supports of positive attitude or belief about the usefulness of Goal Planning and a liking for therapy in general, all contributed to the outcome.

Additional regression equations were examined for the separate influence of the intermediate- versus the individual-level variables (see Table 4.7). As the R^2 figures of .18 and .17 indicate, neither of these sets of variables alone accounted for even half of the variance explained by both types of variables together. Neither type was able to account for the explanatory power of the other group. Further, the regression coefficients for the individual variables were mostly smaller than the coefficients for the same variable in the equation with both sets of variables included. This indicates that controlling for the other level of analysis in this social system was important in order to understand the explanatory influence of either type of variable. The negative coefficient for attitude toward Goal Plans when intermediate-level influences were not controlled seemed to indicate that a more negative attitude was slightly associated with more Goal Plan writing and was consistent with the zero-order correlation coefficient of $-.09$ between number of Goal Plans written and attitude toward Goal Plans. However, in the full equation controlling for the intermediate-level variables, a substantial positive relation between Goal Plan writing and attitude toward Goal Plans was shown, thus confirming the theoretically expected relationship. Both situational and individual characteristics influenced the behavior of these staff members concerning Goal Planning; both types of influence working together were essential to account for the target behavior.

Although the quantitative analyses could not include macro-level variables, since these are essentially constant for all staff members of a single organization, some relationships among the levels can be suggested. As the decision-making processes concerning Goal Planning were described, no overall planning was undertaken to integrate this psychologically oriented therapy system into the supervisory expectations of nurses. The lack of clear supervisory expectations at the unit level, with nurses' actual desires for therapy unrelated to therapy aides' perceptions of their supervisors' expectations, may have derived from this absence of continued planning to facilitate implementation of the innovation. Further, the emphasis of external regulatory agencies on examining records to document maintenance of

TABLE 4.7

Standardized Regression Coefficients for Number of Goal
Plans from Intermediate- and Micro-Level Variables,
Separately and Together, Unit Staff Only (N = 65)

Predictor Variables	(1) All Variables	(2) Intermediate Level Variables	(3) Micro-Level Variables
Intermediate-Level Variables			
Supervisory Expectations-Perceived	.22	.29	
Supervisory Expectations-Actual	.16	.12	
Presence of Routines	.14	.11	
Time on Unit-In Months	.37	.17	
Discussions with Co-workers-Frequency	-.31	-.22	
Micro-Level Variables			
Age	-.35		-.13
Satisfaction with Job	.24		.19
"Professional" Reading	.28		.22
Attitude Toward Goal Plans	.17		-.07
Liking for Therapy	.27		.33
R^2	.40	.18	.17
F	3.58	2.64	2.45
df	10/54	5/59	5/59

physical standards would also push nursing priorities toward
traditional care-oriented activities.

The hierarchical control processes within the nursing service
led to established routines for essential nursing procedures—for
example, giving medication—but did not include carrying out
Goal Plans as an essential part of the unit regimen. Conversely,
the greater autonomy permitted program departments allowed
the department head to establish an orientation toward Goal
Planning for his or her program area; the department head then
set up operating procedures for that staff which were or were
not compatible with Goal Planning. Further, the hierarchical
control processes depended on a downward communication
flow but inhibited upward and perhaps also horizontal communications between units and programs, which may help
account for the low explanatory power of the communication

flow indicators. Because there was only weak coordination among the separate disciplines, individual staff may have been reluctant to initiate discussions of individual residents' problems: There was no ongoing means of negotiating or resolving any inconsistencies of treatment that might be uncovered by such discussions.

The fact that no additional staff resources were added to encourage implementation of Goal Plans, and that existing staff numbers were stretched to cover the opening of several new units, had several probable consequences. It is likely to have led to frequent transfers of therapy aides from one unit to another, resulting in shorter time per therapy aide on any particular unit, which was found to be detrimental to Goal Planning. Staff that felt heavy time pressures to complete essential responsibilities would also have little time to extend informal communications with discipline staff; thus, consistency of Goal Planned treatment was not facilitated. Further, the therapy aides' perception of inadequate staff for important unit responsibilities was likely to have reduced their job satisfaction, thus undermining personal motivation to do Goal Planning. Such perceptions of short staffing were also likely to contribute to the negative influence of discussions with co-workers on the unit; co-workers were unlikely to encourage additional Goal Plan writing if they already felt overloaded with work.

Some influences "from the bottom up" of individual-level variables on intermediate- and macro-level processes can also be suggested, although these effects were likely to be less powerful in the organization as a whole, because the hierarchical control process in this organization did not encourage individual lower-level staff to take initiatives toward change. Yet, such variables as individual beliefs in the efficacy of Goal Planning were highly likely to influence the group norms established on each unit. Further, it is essential to differentiate among individuals at various levels within the organization, for the orientation and beliefs of the individuals who were heads of departments or responsible for decision processes were vitally influential in establishing all the intermediate-level processes. Although behavioral skills were not found to be related to the implementation of this new program, this may have resulted from the lack of support for use of these skills from higher levels. Finally, in spite of strong macro-level and interemediate-level influences operating in this situation, individual differences in orientation toward the job, reflected in liking for therapy and professional reading, remained as substantive predictors. Individual differences were not swamped by situational determinants.

The overall fit of the conceptual model developed in Chapter 2 with the data on Goal Planning at the Developmental Center has revealed substantial explanatory power for the model. The regression equations for both unit staff and program area staff show considerable proportions of variance accounted for, while individual regression coefficients show independent, usually statistically significant, effects for nearly all the intermediate- and individual-level components in the model. Further, the separate equations for these two types of variables show little tendency for any of the variables to adequately account for the explanatory power of any others. Qualitative analysis of macro-level processes has suggested how these processes have influenced the development of intermediate- and micro-level variables in directions which inhibit or facilitate Goal Planning. Implementation or the lack of it in this situation has thus been shown to be the result of the total set of interrelationships occurring within the social system that generated the organization.

5

Assessing the
Token Economy Program

Every organization is unique. Even organizations with similar purposes, regulating environments, and formal internal structures have individual organizational histories, different personnel in key roles, and varied informal working relationships among their staff. Therefore, the question of generalizability of research results arises when a theory of organizational processes is developed and tested from experience in any single organization. In this project, a model of program implementation was developed both from previous literature about implementation and from pilot research undertaken at the Developmental Center. Extensive data to examine the usefulness of the model were collected at the Developmental Center and have been reported in Chapters 3 and 4. But the generalizability of the model remains an open question. Were the processes of implementation found at three organizational levels of the Developmental Center unique to that setting, or would the same processes influence the implementation of other programs in other organizations?

The question of the model's generalizability could be fully addressed only by a large-scale sample of organizations undergoing change, preferably with experimental manipulations of key processes, and detailed observations over time of the changing interrelationships among the components of the model. Nevertheless, additional evidence about the model's usefulness can be generated by additional case studies of organizations attempting to implement new programs. One such case study is reported in this chapter, an examination of a token economy program undertaken in a state mental hospital. Since the scope of the program involved only one ward, the number of staff members participating was too small for quantitative analysis. Therefore, this case study is focused particularly on the macro-level components as they influenced the development of the program over time. The purpose is to examine the interrelationships of the macro-level processes with the intermediate and individual-level processes in order to assess their ability to illuminate program implementation in this setting. A comparison of processes between this study at the Psychiatric Center and the Developmental Center will be deferred to Chapter 6.

THE SETTING

The Psychiatric Center is part of the New York State Department of Mental Hygiene. Founded in the 1860s as an asylum for "inebriates," at the time of this study it was a general purpose state mental hospital housing about 700 patients. Over the past ten years the patient population had been cut by about half, as state-mandated policies of community placement were enforced by reduced budget allocations for inpatient staffing. Physically, the center spreads over a land area of several miles, with a variety of buildings. The present administration building was, in the late nineteenth century, the main hospital, with grey stone walls, dark wood paneling, and high ceilings giving a feeling of shutting out the rest of the world. In sharp contrast, a high-rise geriatrics building about ten years old houses a large number of patients in a modern hospital setting. Buildings of various sizes and ages accommodate the center's major subdivisions, called units.

The token economy program studied here involved only one ward for 22 patients, all female, which was part of the Extended Treatment Unit for long-term institutionalized residents. It was housed in a forbidding looking red brick building with stereotypical heavy-mesh screens covering windows and porches. The ward itself was a rather nondescript set of institutionalized rooms, with drab furniture usually pushed against the walls in which patients sat and stared at an occasional visitor, unless a confrontation between patients created a commotion. The patients were women with histories of long-term hospitalization (average length of stay was 17 years), mostly diagnosed as chronic schizophrenics, many with low measured intelligence and previous unwillingness to participate voluntarily in most recreational or therapeutic programs.

The Token Economy Program was adopted for this ward in February 1977 at a time of general reorganization within the center. Whereas patients had previously been grouped by their home county, with both acute and long-term patients on the same ward, the reorganization during the winter of 1976-1977 regrouped them by type of functional problem. With this concentration of chronic patients on one ward, the possibility of improvement through a highly structured behavioral modification program was suggested by the success of similar programs with chronic patients elsewhere (for example, Ayllon and Azrin, 1968; Atthowe and Krasner, 1968; Kasdin, 1977). Thus, a Token Economy Program (TEP) was adopted on a trial basis for the ward through decision processes to be described further below.

METHODS OF STUDY

The program at the Psychiatric Center was selected as a case study because this center, like the Developmental Center, is a state mental health facility undertaking a psychology-oriented innovation. It was expected that significant features of the environment and of the innovation would be similar to those at the Developmental Center, thus making it possible to focus comparisons on the internal processes surrounding implementation. In addition, the Psychiatric Center was located conveniently in the same community as the Developmental Center. Access for studying the program was readily gained through contact with the chief psychologist in August 1977, about seven months after the program was initiated.

Information to construct this case history was derived mainly from interviews with most of the staff members who had contact with the program, from the deputy director-clinical to therapy aides on the ward. In all, 22 interviews were conducted with 17 different people, including four psychologists, four nurses, five therapy aides, three psychiatrists, and a social worker. Several key staff members were interviewed often during field work at the center, which took place intermittently between August 1977 and February 1978. (In order to preserve confidentiality of responses about individual roles within this small-scale program, the names and specific roles of those involved in key incidents will not be used.) The interviews emphasized open-ended questions, focusing on the components of the implementation model as it applied to the Token Economy. A questionnaire for therapy aides was devised which included some of the same structured-response questions that had been asked at the Developmental Center, but there were too few cases for quantitative analysis.

Additional sources of data about the program included written documents from the center, particularly a program manual for the TEP; informal observation of ward meetings and of daily activities on the ward; and some data about levels of tokens earned and spent and about patient-staff interaction, which were collected by the psychology staff. When this investigation of implementation processes was planned in association with the psychology staff, it was anticipated that additional data would be available on individuaal staff members' distribution of tokens from a daily recording by each therapy aide of token slips given out. However, therapy aides refused to do this additional data recording and were supported in their refusal by the nursing supervisors, on the grounds that therapy aides had too much paperwork to do to add any more. Further, no data were collected on patient behaviors that were supposed to be modified by the Token Economy, so little hard evidence is available about either the progress of program implementation or the outcomes for patient behavior. This conflict between psychologists and ward staff over collection of data was not an isolated incident, but in fact symbolizes a continuing tension over role definitions within the program, a conflict which will be further analyzed below. The lack of adequate data collection not only affected this attempt to investigate implementation processes but also prevented accurate feedback to any of the staff working in this program.

Analysis of the interview materials collected on the Token Economy was qualitative only, by grouping together and then examining the comments of various participants pertaining to the components of the model. The discussion is therefore necessarily a subjective interpretation of the status and processes of implementation up to the time the field interviews were completed, with just a few notes on its further history. Yet, there was enough convergence among the participants in their accounts of basic events concerning the TEP to confirm that many of the problematic issues discussed here were not the idiosyncratic perceptions of a single observer. However, the application of the social systems model of implementation developed here can reveal organizational processes affecting this innovation that were not always apparent to the participants.

THE PROGRAM AND
ITS LEVEL OF IMPLEMENTATION

The ideas underlying a token economy have been used for centuries in the development of symbolic exchange media such as money. However, within the last twenty years, behavioral psychologists have experimentally developed procedures for creating more highly structured environments to modify the behavior of people, such as chronic mental patients or retarded individuals, who do not exhibit socially appropriate responses to normal patterns of social interactions and reinforcements. The term "token economy" refers to the use of paper or plastic tokens as immediate reinforcers for desired behavior. As developed in Ayllon and Azrin's (1968) well-known creation of a token economy for a ward of chronic mental patients, the focus of this program was to design a total environment that would motivate psychiatric patients. While researchers following up Ayllon and Azrin's innovation have developed a wide variety of reinforcers and techniques (see the review by Kazdin, 1977), the essence of a token economy remains the establishment of reinforcing consequences contingent upon defined socially appropriate behaviors.

The manual written as a program guide for the TEP at the Psychiatric Center clearly focuses on these essential elements in defining the program:

> A TEP is a motivational system in which specific undesirable behaviors can be modified and new adaptive behaviors can be taught . . . The TEP is a structured system which allows for the standardized delivery of rewards.

The TEP was planned to utilize paper tokens to reinforce patient behaviors in terms of four major areas of short-term goals: (a) self-maintenance and personal hygiene, (b) reduction of extreme bizarre or agressive behavior, (c) increasing independence and personal responsibility by attendance and participation in appropriate programs and recreational activities, and (d) resocialization in interpersonal and communication skills. These immediate goals were intended to work toward the longer-term goal of family care placement with specially trained family home operators who would continue and extend the structured environment developed around the token economy. These goals were outlined in the Token Economy Program Manual dated March 1, 1977, which also spelled out some operational details for the program, such as setting up a ward store of reinforcing items, listing tokens to be earned for specific behaviors, and developing individual treatment plans by joint planning of the psychologists and therapy aides.

However, no clear operational definition of implementation is included in the manual that specifies detailed behavioral roles for staff participants in the program. How to determine when the program was implemented as intended was left undefined. Therefore, in order to assess the degree of program implementation for this study, a list of program elements was developed from interviews with the participating psychologists and by examining the program manual; the list was confirmed with some modifications by the center's chief psychologist. The program elements are as follows:

(1) Distribution of tokens to all patients for defined on-ward behaviors; specifically, a standard list of daily activities.

(2) Distribution of tokens by the staff of recreational and therapeutic programs for patient attendance and participation.

(3) Operation of the ward store at specified times daily, with selection of merchandise for purchase with tokens that patients would find attractive as back-up reinforcers.

(4) Operation of a voluntary "small-jobs" system on the ward, in which patients can earn extra tokens by contracting for weekly duty on specified jobs.

(5) Treatment planning for each individual patient jointly by a psychologist and therapy aide at least once every three months. This draft plan was to be submitted to the team meeting for modification and approval. Individual behavioral modification procedures using tokens were to be incorporated into these plans, as determined by the team meeting.

(6) A pattern of staff-patient interaction incorporating a high ratio of positive to negative interactions (such as praise, approval, and interest exhibited by the staff members instead of corrections and prohibitions).

(7) Appropriate staff behavior for intervention in crises, such as fights between patients or aggressive outbursts. The staff member intervening should act crisply and decisively to control the immediate situation, but should avoid counseling or conversation during the actual incident (thus to avoid giving positive reinforcement for disruptive behaviors).

(8) Development of Family Care homes to continue a structured, reinforcing environment for patients whose behaviors improved sufficiently to allow such placement.

However, since such a list of TEP elements was never developed by the program staff, their attempts to elicit change at particular points in the program's history were often focused on specific elements, rather than considering the progress of the program as a whole. For example, several psychologists, when interviewed, emphasized the problems of stimulating the therapy aides' capability to write individual treatment plans, but placed little emphasis on the development of on-ward token distribution routines. Conversely, therapy aides seemed to view the token economy as entirely concerned with the distribution and redemption of the tokens and did not consider individual treatment planning a part of the program, since this was also required in the remaining wards of the hospital.

The level of TEP implementation can best be described by recounting a history of its development and problems up to the point at which this research was conducted. As mentioned previously, the program was initiated in January 1977 at a time of general patient reorganization by the suggestions of psychiatrists in administrative positions. Although the psychologists in general were not enthusiastic about becoming involved in the program, one psychologist, who will be called Psychologist A, was available for a new project and felt that developing a Token Economy would be a professional challenge. With the support of the chief psychologist, Psychologist A wrote the program manual, arranged informal permission to begin the program, and was appointed program coordinator. An inservice training program for ward staff was developed around training modules; most ward staff reported attending most sections of the training around March 1977. Just as the TEP was to start on the ward, Psychologist A learned that her job classification with the state, which had been temporary, was denied permanent standing, and she resigned rather than accepting a lower job status. The start of the TEP on the ward was then delayed until Psychologist B reluctantly accepted the position of coordinator.

The distribution of tokens on the ward started in May 1977, but other parts of the program—particularly individual treatment planning—lagged behind over the summer, as psychologists and other staff members' vacations prevented close, informal working relationships from developing between therapy aides and psychologists. Obtaining supplies for the ward store also became troublesome, for the expected variety of free articles from Volunteer Service was not available, and a flexible use of the budgeted fifty dollars per month was hindered by Business Office regulations.

Near the end of the summer, as this research was beginning, Psychologist B attempted to develop better data-recording procedures on the unit but was rebuffed by the unit staff. When he tried to have his role as program coordinator clarified by seeking "line authority" from the deputy director-clinical, Psychologist B was told that his authority was the same as any other member of the team. Since supervisory authority over therapy aides' activities was firmly held by the nursing hierarchy, this meant that staff behavior in the Token Economy was still under the nurses' direction, rather than following the psychologists' views of behaviors necessary for the TEP. With this lack of authority to create on-ward changes, Psychologist B assumed a detached role of advisor and program evaluator rather than functioning as an active manager or facilitator of the program.

Problems of inadequate supplies for the ward store continued through the fall. In addition, ward staff were plagued by individual differences in patients' levels of functioning, such that some patients earned many tokens quickly and bought up, then horded, items such as sodas when these were available intermittently from the ward store. Then other patients who might have been motivated by the system had nothing to buy, while a few patients were perceived by ward staff as too regressed to have any interest in tokens. Ward staff initiated a change in the program in November 1977 to begin a "levels" system in which some patients would receive tokens for helping other patients with daily tasks such as dressing and bed-making. While this was enthusiastically supported at first by therapy aides and, reportedly, by patients, this, too, lapsed after several weeks when conflicts arose between patient helpers and recipients. By the time most interviews were conducted with the ward staff in

December 1977, the token economy was widely perceived as operating only in pro forma fashion, particularly due to inadequate supplies of reinforcers for token exchange. One therapy aide's assessment was, "Now its like a tire that's gone flat."

Although a revival of the TEP might have been initiated when the budget for the ward store was increased to $200 per month in February 1978, this financial support was apparently not sufficient to overcome the organizational problems that will be detailed here. In April 1978, Psychologist B, still nominally program coordinator, recommended to the deputy director-clinical that the program be terminated or that he be given sufficient authority to create the changes necessary to implement it adequately. A summary of these major events in the TEP is listed in Table 5.1 for further reference as organizational processes are analyzed.

This history has summarized the conclusion of most staff members interviewed regarding implementation of the program: It was a failure. This opinion was stated early in the fall by the psychologists involved and was echoed by the ward staff in December. Yet, examination of the elements of the TEP previously listed reveals that some of the elements were being carried out, even while the program was pronounced dead. For example, the distribution of tokens for daily ward activities and attendance at programs was carried out routinely from May 1977 until December of that year. But whether this staff activity had any influence on patient behaviors is unknown, since no baseline data were collected before the start of the TEP, nor were there careful records of patient behaviors that might have been modified by the use of tokens. Further, the small jobs system was established and operated during the summer of 1977, but therapy aides' supervision of it waned when there were no effective reinforcers in the ward store, and neither nurses nor psychologists actively supported their efforts.

Psychologists' implementation efforts were focused mainly on the changes in the individual treatment planning process, in which immediate behavioral goals for each patient were to be developed and individual programs using tokens to reinforce

TABLE 5.1
Chronology of Major Events Concerning the Token Economy Program

January 1977	Proposal for Token Economy from center psychiatrists.
February 1977	Psychology department and Psychologist A became committed to developing TEP; Psychologist A designated as program coordinator.
March 1977	Development of TEP Manual. In-service training for ward staff. Formal approval of TEP by Cabinet Committee.
April 1977	Resignation of Psychologist A, replacement by Psychologist B.
May 1977	Start of TEP on ward.
June 1977	Nurse Administrator A transferred, replaced by Nurse Administrator B.
September 1977	Psychologist B requests formal authority as program coordinator; is refused.
November 1977	"Levels" of Patients designated for different contingencies in TEP.
February 1978	Budget for ward store increased from $50 to $200 per month.
April 1978	Psychologist B recommends termination of TEP to Cabinet Committee.

particular behaviors planned as appropriate. Before the initiation of the TEP, and in other wards of the center, individual treatment plans were usually written in weekly team meetings directed by the ward psychiatrist. Within the TEP, this procedure was to be changed to have the primary therapist for a patient due for a treatment plan (ward therapy aides were assigned as primary therapists) contact the psychologist for that patient (several of the psychology staff were to participate in this phase of the TEP) to jointly draft a treatment plan which would incorporate the behavioral modification techniques of the TEP. This treatment planning procedure was initiated by Psychologist A and was started on the ward even before her resignation.

Then, with the delays and confusion over starting the TEP and with staff schedules interrupted by summer vacations, this joint planning procedure did not become established as a routine. In addition, some of the plans that had been developed under psychologists' guidance were later returned for revision by the center's Utilization Review Committee on the grounds that they lacked proper documentation of the patients' psychotic symptoms. This committee was responsible for assuring that continued stay was necessary for each patient and, within the medical theory of mental illness prevailing at the center, required justification in terms of psychotic symptoms. Although such documentation easily could have been included in the treatment plans within the TEP, the fact that the plans developed by psychologists neglected it damaged the credibility of the psychologists in their interactions with nurses and therapy aides. Thus, by November, therapy aides were no longer contacting psychologists for assistance in developing treatment plans, although no formal decision had authorized this change. Instead, the team meetings reverted to the center's usual system of writing the plans in lengthy meetings chaired by the psychiatrist.

The fact that psychologists' implementation efforts focused on the process for individual treatment planning perhaps prevented them from putting more emphasis on the parts of the TEP which were being carried out: the distribution and redemption of tokens by therapy aides and off-ward program staff. Although the routines for this staff activity were established, there was little emphasis by either psychologists or administrators on the behavioral effects this activity might be having on the patients. The essential characteristic of a Token Economy— to establish a total environment with structured behavior-reward contingencies for patients—seems to have been forgotten in the controversies over leadership roles and supply problems for the ward store.

To summarize this description of the program and its lack of implementation, the TEP was developed very rapidly and carefully in its early stages, but floundered following the change of psychologists as program coordinator. Although some elements of the program were established as part of the ward routine, these distributional aspects were not closely connected with an adequate supply of reinforcing items or events or with records of any changes in patient behavior. Thus, the initial work of establishing this much of the economy was not followed by any feedback data on the results of staff efforts, nor was it viewed positively as a first phase of implementing the total program. Instead, there were early feelings of discouragement with aspects of the program which were not well implemented, such as the individual treatment planning and psychologists' inability to direct therapy aides' interaction with patients. By the time this research was conducted, the TEP existed in name only; a situation which apparently had not changed several months later when the coordinating psychologist recommended termination of the program.

ANALYSIS OF IMPLEMENTATION: THE MACRO LEVEL

Psychiatric Center staff members' explanations for the ongoing implementation problems with the TEP tended to center on one or more of the issues described above—the lack of continuous and varied items as reinforcers for the ward store, whether patients admitted to the ward were appropriate for this program, the failure of another staff member to support the program adequately, or conflicts in authority which blocked necessary changes in ward procedures. In one sense, each of these explanations was probably correct, for these issues were real and serious blocks to fuller implementation of the program. On the other hand, no one seemed to view implementation as involving the total organizational system that surrounded this particular ward. No plans were developed to coordinate the various changes that would be needed to make the program effective; no one had clear responsibility for managing the numerous details which would support or undermine the program. As the discussion to follow will show, the failure to implement this program was related to many aspects of all three levels of organizational processes within the center; and no one problem or person was *the* key to fuller implementation.

DECISION PROCESSES

As indicated, the TEP was initiated at a time of widespread patient reorganization, following the interest expressed in the idea by the center's clinical administrators, who were psychiatrists. Although the psychologists agreed that it was an appropriate type of program for the problems of the chronic patients on that ward, several psychologists interviewed expressed their personal lack of interest in being involved. Said one, "It's a deadly, dull, boring program—not what I got into psychology for." The fact that it was started at all was due to the initiative of Psychologist A, who had been employed at the center less than a year but was interested in tackling the challenge of a token economy. Thus, the Psychology Department became officially committed to the program in support of the professional interest of one of its staff members, who, because of a state civil service ruling, was forced to resign less than three months later. The administrator who had expressed early interest in the program did facilitate securing official approval and some financial support for it, but did not take an active role in the details of implementation.

After Psychologist A resigned from the center, no one involved in the decision to begin the TEP had a personal stake in pushing for its implementation. Psychologist B was appointed "Coordinator" by the chief psychologist, apparently simply because someone had to fill the role and Psychologist B had previous experience working with those patients and not too many other responsibilities at the time. When his attempts failed to obtain formal authority over ward staff, Psychologist B limited his personal involvement to fulfilling formal requirements for attending team meetings, doing paperwork, and providing program evaluation; however, he felt that other efforts on the program were not worthwhile, since he had no control over staff. Other professionals working with the unit believed that it was the Psychology Department's responsibility and/or that it would not help these patients' incurable problems and so did not take personal initiative for solving implementation problems.

CONTROL PROCESSES

As indicated above, the decision process to begin a token economy took place almost entirely at the top administrative levels of the center, the sole exception being involvement of the interested psychology staff members. Ward-level staff were not consulted, even though several of them had worked on a token economy ward about eight years previously. Considerable dissatisfaction with this centralized type of control was revealed by one nurse when she was asked how it was decided to have the TEP on the ward:

> I don't really know how it was decided. . . . They just told me it would be done. In fact, I should have been involved with this decision, since I am on the program review committee for this unit. The committee is supposed to decide on issues of program change for the unit, but this [TEP] was just presented to us as a finished document.

Further, the ward staff was simply assigned to work on the ward by the usual Nursing Service procedures, even though most token economies are developed by staff volunteering for this type of program.

In spite of this centralized procedure controlling major program changes, little centralized direction or coordination was exercised over the daily operation of the program. The unit administrator explained,

> I don't try to keep close tabs on everything that happens on the wards. That's not my style. I have general supervisory capacity over the medical matters, but each discipline has its own direct line of supervision. . . . I let them operate on their own.

The multiple disciplines supposedly contributing to the treatment team at the ward level—physicians, nurses, psychologists, social workers, and so forth—each had their own professional leadership and orientation. These supervisory patterns were not disturbed with the initiation of a token economy. Therapy aides, who had the primary patient contact, were supervised through the nursing hierarchy, while responsibility for pre-scribing each patient's treatment was held by the ward psychia-trists. In most wards, the psychologist was an auxiliary advisor—a "satellite," as described by one of them—who had no power to prescribe or proscribe staff behavior on the ward. It was this peripheral role position that psychologists aimed to change by boosting input into the treatment planning process and by seeking "line authority" over some aspects of staff behavior.

Since the token economy was originally designed by psychol-ogists, it is reasonable that the psychologists should have a leading role in its implementation here. Yet, interviews with psychologists often left the impression that they were using the token economy to obtain increased overall power for their discipline, rather than seeking only sufficient authority to implement the program. Psychologists perceived nurses as un-willing to change the ward routines to those necessary to implement the program: "They say they want to play football, but they don't want to do it on a football field," explained one psychologist. But ward staff, both nurses and therapy aides, complained that the psychologist often was not available to support their efforts. "We needed a coach, to be around as a loyal believer," said one therapy aide. It may be that nurses perceived the psychologist as trying to be quarterback by calling the individual plays, while they believed what was needed was a coach who would supply technical information and support for the team's ball-carrying efforts.

Thus, underlying the daily implementation problems of this program were unresolved power conflicts between disciplines. Such conflicts were reported to be pervasive through the center and probably had a basis in the long-term decline of influence for Nursing Services (which had previously operated a very influential nursing school at the center), the theoretical chal-lenges to the prevailing medical model of mental illness, and the increasing numbers and influence of psychologists. Establish-ment of the token economy had no lasting provision for re-solving any of these role authority conflicts, because the admin-istrative staff, who might have mediated at least to establish formal areas of authority for the conflicting disciplines maintained a "hands-off" policy. When interviewed within the same month, a nurse and a physician each specified that he had the responsibility of "team leader," while at the same time the psychologist was formally designated "program coordinator." With such confused lines of authority, new aspects of the token economy, such as collecting frequency data on patient behavior or reserving outings as rewards to be purchased with tokens, could not be readily instituted but had to be elaborately negotiated with each different discipline, if they were to be done at all.

In summary, some control processes in this situation were centralized, such as the basic decisions on type of program to be developed, while in other respects the situation was decentralized, such as the laissez-faire policy regarding the resolution of role conflicts between various disciplines. The lack of means for coordination among disciplines most often left each discipline to go in its own direction. A "total structured environment" that would motivate new patient behaviors in a token economy demanded a level of interdisciplinary coordination that was not present prior to the TEP and was not perceived as essential by the administrators who might have provided it. Thus, the control processes which established the program did not engender either individual commitment of individuals to work together informally or formal coordination of the diverse disciplinary interests which make up a treatment team.

OBTAINING RESOURCES

While some attention was given in developing this program to assembling appropriate resources, problems recurred in terms of all three resources areas—staff, time, and financial support. The major problem concerning staffing were the rapid changes in professional personnel. The departure of Psychologist A was a key loss to the program, because the interest and initiative of this person had sparked the adoption of the TEP. In addition, the administrative nurse who had contributed to establishing the ward routines in the spring had been a temporary replacement for the permanent administrator, who returned in June. The long-term ward psychiatrist retired in July and was replaced by a young, foreign-born psychiatrist who had just completed his residency. Two other changes in ward nursing staff took place in the ten months after adoption of the TEP on the ward. These changes in the professional staff also interrupted any potential for developing a cohesive treatment team to solve other implementation problems.

Whether the ward was more heavily staffed because of the TEP than other similar wards was reported diversely by different informants. Psychologist A stated that the ward did receive one additional nurse and several more therapy aides than normal, but other psychologists reported that no additional staff were assigned to the ward, even though most accounts of other token economies report higher than usual staff ratios. Nurses also complained that the number of therapy aides assigned to the ward—six during the day shift and three for the evening—was inadequate for attempting individual on-ward therapy with 22 patients. The number of staff on the ward at any one time would usually be less than the number assigned, due to rotating days off, vacation time, or any staff illness. Whatever the absolute level in comparison with either other token economies or other wards at the center, an inadequate number of staff was perceived by the ward staff to be a serious block to increased individualized use of tokens.

The level of staffing relates closely to the perennial resource problem, a lack of time for new duties. This was the objection given by ward staff to the psychologist's request for more data collection on the ward, although how much of this staff resistance was simply avoiding additional job duties rather than actual time pressures could not be determined without close behavioral observation of the use of staff time on the ward. The fact that this program finally began operating on the ward just before the summer vacation period also meant that psychologists' time for contributing to individual treatment plans was in short supply, so therapy aides became discouraged in their attempts to initiate any joint treatment planning. Considering time longitudinally, the rapid start of the TEP by Psychologist A probably prevented dissenters from organizing delay but also prevented the development of a cohesive working team to continue problem-solving efforts when the key person was suddenly withdrawn. Then the delays in the date of on-ward use of tokens dampened the enthusiasm for the program which had been sparked in the training period. Thus, time resources played a part in the difficulties facing this program.

The resource problem considered the most serious by most of those interviewed was the lack of adequate financial support to purchase supplies for the ward store. The token economy manual proposing the program requested a budget of $50.00 per month for the store, or about $2.25 per patient; it indicated also that some articles could be obtained from donations made available to Volunteer Services. Whether it was originally thought that this amount would be adequate or whether this was all that could be squeezed on short notice out of a tight budget was not clear from the interviews, but by early fall it was cited as a major stumbling block by several staff members:

> Sometimes there is an embarrassing lack of reinforcing items in the store. We used to get coffee for patient coffee breaks from the kitchens, but now we have to buy even that. [Comment of a psychologist.]

> Supplies for the token store were a problem when we first started, and still are. We're limited to fifty dollars a month, which is only six cents a day per patient. Some patients save tokens for three weeks, then in one week all the new supplies are gone. Then you can't expect the patients to participate. . . . The administration wants to see the program go, but don't give us the stuff to work with. [From a therapy aide.]

Although several staff members mentioned possibilities for obtaining reinforcers without cost, such as using outings or extra movies or including clothing supplied through the state's usual system for indigent patients, no one took the initiative to overcome obstacles to utilize these resources. By December, the ward psychiatrist and Psychologist B had joined forces in a formal request for increasing the budget to $200.00 per month. This was finally approved in early February but was not enough to revitalize the program. Although the $200.00 in additional supplies were received in March, and again in late April, by this time the higher functioning patients had a large surplus of tokens and bought up the new supplies rapidly. Even this large increase in budget did not assure a continuous supply of reinforcers.

This discussion of resources has revealed a number of problems in resources of staff, time, and money. Yet, the program did receive some attention to these problems by the center's administrators, who were able to allocate substantially higher financial support, though not without delay. Further, ideas were present for alleviating the serious shortage of reinforcers, but no staff member felt responsible for initiating contacts to obtain the supplies from other parts of the center. The resource problems were more likely to be serving as justifications for inaction by various participants, who were discouraged by the disciplinary conflicts and lack of patient progress, than really insurmountable barriers to fuller implementation.

RELATIONS WITH THE ENVIRONMENT

A ward of chronic mental patients has few direct supporters to bring political pressure on staff attempting an innovative treatment program. But this relative insulation from public opinion was balanced by a heavy weight of regulations from state and federal agencies, which helped to sink the TEP. For example, state civil service procedures sharply interrupted the development of the economy when Psychologist A was denied permanent appointment in the psychology classification to which she had been provisionally appointed by the chief psychologist nearly a year earlier. The crucial personal commitment for a program coordinator with a professional stake in managing the implementation details was thus lost to the TEP. Civil service regulations also may have influenced the failure to solicit volunteer therapy aides and nurses as ward staff, for if these were categorized as "new positions" within the center, regulations required that they be openly posted. But, according to one informant, the Personnel Office was reluctant to classify jobs as new whenever possible because the open selection process often generated complaints and grievances which required complicated personnel procedures to resolve. Thus, the positions were not openly posted for volunteers, but were simply filled by the normal processes of staff assignment by the head of Nursing Services.

A second aspect of the TEP in which outside regulations played a role is the emphasis of all the professional staff on individual treatment plans for each patient. Both state regulations and federal financial reimbursement procedures required such individual plans, which were to document the psychiatric symptoms justifying continued inpatient status, and had to be signed by the psychiatrist as head of the treatment team. Thus, it is understandable that the psychologists emphasized procedures for developing individual plans when designing the TEP, both to fulfill the external regulations and to mesh with the treatment expectations of the medically trained psychiatrists and nurses. But this emphasis probably diverted psychologists' attention from wardwide routines utilizing the token economy which might have been more feasible to implement given the level of staffing and added to the emphasis on "paperwork" which ward staff felt oppressive.

Several other elements of the regulatory environment probably had indirect influences on this program. For example, the center was visited by an inspection team from the Joint Commission for Accreditation of Hospitals (JCAH) in early September, a semiofficial agency which had approved only a one-year renewal of accreditation the previous year. Higher-level administrators were preoccupied during the late summer with preparations for this inspection, which was expected to focus not on the details of carrying out a treatment program but on compliance with regulations concerning aspects such as cleanliness and medications. Said one administrator, when asked if the JCAH inspection affected the functioning of the TEP:

> The TEP got shoved. Our overriding concern [during the late summer] was with preparing the report for them, and in shoring up weak areas. The TEP ward is the only ward with a written manual, and other areas needed buttressing much more.

The JCAH inspection did lead to the normal two-year accreditation approval, but the authority conflicts of the TEP professionals, which came to a head at about the same time, remained unresolved.

Another environmental element in the background of this program is the legal controversy over "patients' rights," which some staff interpreted as preventing the use as reinforcers within the TEP of privileges freely available to patients on other wards. Without leeway to use any deprivation to tap any basic primary reinforcers, some staff felt that some of the most regressed patients would not respond to the use of tokens. Further, ward staff felt they were caught in a "double-bind" situation by the emphasis on patients' rights: If they watched the patients closely, they were "de-humanizing"; but if they did not, and a patient wandered off or exhibited inappropriate behavior in public, they would be guilty of "poor supervision." Consequently, ward staff tended to follow rules and supervisory directions closely, rather than exercising individual initiative for activities with patients that might lead to trouble. Thus, environmental pressures were felt in subtle ways by various levels of staff in the TEP. Civil service regulations, requirements for individual treatment plans, accreditation inspections, and advocation of "patients' rights," all intended in the abstract to improve patient care in mental hospitals, in this concrete case helped to undermine the implementation processes for a new type of treatment program.

In summary, the overall influence of macro-level organizational components on the implementation of the TEP has been shown to be strong. The decision processes creating the program were instigated by the prodding of one dynamic individual but did not involve the first-line implementors of the program or create a strong team of supporters among the professional staff who were later to be responsible for the program. The mixture of centralized and laissez-faire control processes did little to resolve jurisdictional and leadership conflicts among professional staff, which needed to be resolved in order to establish the consistent environment of behavior-reinforcement contingencies of a token economy. Scarcity of resources, particularly for adequate staffing and for financial support of the ward store, as well as pressures from environmental regulations pulling away from efforts on the TEP, created problems for the program for which control patterns of responsibility and authority were inadequate. Although intermediate- and individual-level components were also related to the implementation failure of this program, the direction for several of these components was set by the overall organization culture exhibited in the macro-level components.

INTERMEDIATE-LEVEL PROCESSES

SUPERVISORY EXPECTATIONS

The head nurse of the TEP ward was viewed as not in favor of the program by other nurses, psychologists, and at least four out of five therapy aides interviewed. She herself expressed doubts about the likely effectiveness of the program and emphasized the difficulty of obtaining the essential consistency of interaction when patients and staff were frequently shifted off and on the ward. Although other nursing administrators gave somewhat greater support to starting the TEP, they also sometimes refused to direct therapy aides to undertake essential new activities, such as collecting data on either patient or staff behavior. It was clear, then, that the direct supervision of therapy aides did not include strong expectations for creative contributions to the token economy, although the ward routines were modified to include daily distribution and redemption of tokens.

Frequent changes in nurses assigned to the ward also meant that several key staff members did not attend the training sessions explaining the learning theory principles behind a token economy. Then they were likely to exhibit interactions with patients that were counter to learning principles and which would model inappropriate behaviors to therapy aides. For example, a nurse new to the ward mentioned that she spent much time "counseling patients, trying to keep peace between them," and giving "extra attention to head off potential problems," behaviors that might be reinforcing patients' aggressive outbursts, which the TEP was intended to reduce. Similarly, the lack of support for data-collecting was justified by nursing staff as protecting the therapy aides from additional unnecessary work; the nurses apparently did not view information about the results of the TEP as an essential part of the program.

Supervisory links between the professionals on the treatment team and their disciplinary heads were no more strongly supportive of the TEP. Higher-level medical staff stated that the program was a psychology-oriented effort that the psychologist who was formally program coordinator must "sell" to the rest of the staff in order to stimulate the necessary "enthusiastic involvement of staff" to make the TEP work. These medical hierarchy supervisors, who provided direction for the physicians and nurses, appeared to view work motivation even of lower-level therapy aides as primarily internal rather than responsive to external direction. They viewed the program difficulties as problems of "getting interest from the staff," rather than of providing explicit direction for changing work routines. Even the chief psychologist did not appear to put much pressure on Psychologist B to work informally on the problems preventing fuller implementing. Apparently believing that the absence of line authority to direct the program and the lack of support from other disciplines had doomed the program from the start, the chief psychologist did not exert influence on a colleague to get him to try new tactics of interaction with the other staff. Thus, supervisory expectations at all levels of the center were at best ambivalent about the TEP and did not provide firm direction for either daily routines or program management.

STANDARD OPERATING ROUTINES

Some changes in on-ward routines were initiated which contributed to the partial implementation of the TEP. As indicated previously, therapy aides did distribute tokens for daily activities such as bed-making and appropriate dressing, and redeemed them for ward store items (when available) and for going off the ward for free recreational time. These changes in ward procedures were brought about early with the support of supervising nurses, and appear to have been viewed by therapy aides as exchanges in their work duties rather than additions to them. When asked how the TEP changed her job, one therapy aide replied:

> Well, it lessened the laundry job at first, when patients were doing their own laundry for token earnings. They also began to dump the garbage and clean up dishes from the coffee breaks. But we had extra duties in giving out tokens and writing records.

The initial changes in ward routines thus seem to have been accepted rather easily by therapy aides, especially since some of their previous cleaning tasks were taken over by patients.

This focus on gradual changes in daily routines was lost in the previously discussed emphasis on individual treatment plans, which was itself a standard procedure for the clinically trained psychologists and psychiatrists. In addition, the attempt to add new, disliked duties in the form of paperwork to collect data, which therapy aides viewed as neither beneficial to the patients nor as contributing to their work, was successfully resisted by the ward staff. Other changes in ward routines affecting the TEP were started only when they were proposed by the ward staff, such as their grouping of patients into several "levels" of participation in the program. One nurse assessed the development of the program:

> They moved too fast on individual treatment plans to let the therapy aides keep up. . . . If it had stayed simple, then gradually added things, such as emphasizing the patients' daily living needs, it could have worked better.

Therapy aides' orientation to their jobs focused on the daily routines and rules to be followed. Three out of five therapy aides interviewed said there was a known routine, with other assignments written into the daily work schedule by the head nurse. The remaining therapy aides put more emphasis on the disruptions caused by patient outbursts or a need for trips outside. Although the therapy aides seemed to like the idea of contributing to treatment plans from their daily close experience in working with the patients, they did not see themselves as therapists individually responsible for carrying out behavior modification therapy. In short, when the TEP focused on ward routines that involved dropping some duties while adding others, it was more successful; however, when new tasks were added to the job role, or individual initiative and creativity by therapy aides was required rather than changes in the routines, it was not.

A second type of influence of standard operating procedures on this program affecting one ward is that few changes were made in the standard procedures for all wards just to accommodate the new program. One psychologist stated:

> The administration doesn't want to make exceptions to the general rules for one special program. Then other programs would want exceptions, and they'd have to get involved in the daily operating details of several programs.

One example of how this tendency affected the TEP was that the nursing personnel responsible for assigning patients to specific wards tried to even out assignments of very disturbed patients over the wards, so that no single ward was disrupted more than others by patient outbursts. Therefore, the TEP ward got at least its share of aggressive patients, even if they were not appropriate for the program. Several staff thought that more disruptive patients were assigned to this ward because it was one of the only locked wards (it was locked so that tokens could be collected for the privilege of outside recreation).

A second example of the influence of centerwide SOPs is that the $50-per-month allotment for ward store supplies was not available as a lump sum for the program coordinator to simply purchase a variety of merchandise. Instead, it had to be used via purchase orders to the Business Office, which wanted bulk orders of only a few kinds of things each month, and frequently resulted in delay in the arrival of the supplies. A further example is that several recreational activities were not permitted as back-up reinforcers because they were routinely available to all other patients at the center. The standard procedure for individual treatment planning has already been discussed. Thus, the influence of standard operating routines of the center as a whole created additional problems for a shaky program. While some on-ward routines were changed sufficiently to allow at least token implementation of the program, these openings were not followed up by further gradual changes in ward routines.

TECHNICAL REQUIREMENTS

As the preceding discussion of operating routines has implied, the technical requirements for the TEP partly involved fully specified changes in ward routines, such as the number of tokens to be distributed for specific activities or small jobs, and partly individual plans requiring details to be created by the implementors—the therapy aides with assistance from the treatment team professionals. The fully specified aspects were more easily implemented, since they were consistent with the "doing what you're told to do" job orientation of the therapy aides. In contrast, attempting to stimulate and train therapy aides to design treatment policies and individual on-ward therapy programs required greater role changes than occurred, and perhaps more than these individuals were capable of, given their educational backgrounds (see the section on behavioral skills below).

A fairly extensive in-service training program was conducted to introduce ward staff to the principles and procedures of a token economy. The training program contained ten modules of about four hours each, so that training times and modules could be worked around ward staff schedules. Even with the built-in flexibility, the ward's head nurse reported that many staff missed several sections of the training, since they were not entirely relieved of their other duties to attend training. The content was reported by psychologists to be "mostly didactic and demonstration" sessions on behavior modification and the principles of a token economy, with some sessions using assertion training for stimulating more appropriate interaction with patients. Psychologists involved in the training specified that it was meant as an initial exposure only; further learning was to take place later in one-to-one interaction with psychologists while drafting individual treatment plans.

When these individual sessions waned in frequency and further in-service training contemplated for the fall was not carried out, the therapy aides' technical skills were never sufficiently developed to match the technical requirements of the program. When interviewed eight to nine months following the training sessions, therapy aides were vague in their memories of the content of these sessions, but were unanimous in their expression of needs for more training, particularly about "the specifics of dealing with *these* patients, not patients with other types of problems, like we saw in the films."

In addition to the training sessions, the detailed token economy manual was intended by its author as both a program proposal to secure official approval for beginning the program and a continuing reference guide to implementing the program. To attempt to serve these dual purposes in one document was probably counterproductive, for it was written at a level of complexity and abstraction that seemed too difficult, even intimidating, for the therapy aides to refer to in their daily work. Thus, to the extent that the technical requirements for the TEP were spelled out in detail, these aspects were at least initially carried out on the ward. But for those aspects requiring contributions from individual therapy aides, the training sessions, program manual, and other forms of technical assistance were insufficient to bring about the necessary fundamental role changes.

COMMUNICATION FLOW

The previous discussion of the lack of control processes to resolve interdisciplinary conflicts underscores the fact that communication among the team members supposedly working together on the TEP was not open or frank. Particularly among psychologists and nurses, rivalries and grievances festered under the surface of amiable daily relations, with no mediating mechanism to air complaints or clarify role responsibilities. A history of such conflict within the center led the psychologists to propose and develop the TEP without participation from nurses or other disciplines. One psychologist related this period as follows:

> Previously, the psychology staff had tried to get them [the ward staff] on our side, but with little success. This time, we went in like gangbusters, and caught them off guard. I simply called the charge nurse and came over to the ward and told them we would be doing the program. They had never heard of me and didn't expect it. . . . I made the worst possible impression.

To avoid expected objections and delays in starting the program, this one-way communication tactic was used to introduce the program. Later developments did little to increase productive communication, for each discipline blamed others for the recurring implementation problems.

While Psychologist A spent much of her time in the token economy ward after this surprise introduction and might have been able to build open communication channels by frequent, informal interchange, the confusion after she left, plus the reassignment of a supervising nurse and the ward physician, disrupted any openings toward freer communication that might have occurred. Psychologist B did not routinely spend much time on the TEP ward, but instead presented suggested ideas in monthly team meetings. While therapy aides and nurses said he was helpful when they asked him a specific question, nearly all ward staff said they wished he was in the ward more often, to get to know the patients on a daily basis and help work out details of the token system. The psychologist was not available often enough to be a ready source of technical assistance, nor did he function as an informal source of support for therapy aides to counter the lack of direct supervisory support for the program.

Communication links for this program were thus not made between supervisory levels or among disciplines. Although therapy aides stated that their communications with staff of the program areas were good and that program staff supported the TEP by distributing tokens to patients for attending, this linkage was not a central enough aspect of the total TEP to bring about successful implementation.

WORK GROUP NORMS

Little evidence is directly available about the content or operation of work group norms among the therapy aides, but therapy aides' comments about their co-workers' feelings toward the program were mostly negative. Several said they felt confused about how it would work after the training sessions, and that several staff were skeptical whether it would "reach" many of "these patients." It is also likely that the staff's observed custom of sitting together talking and drinking coffee in the staff room when not on an assigned duty would discourage individual initiative toward interaction with patients. By the time of the interviews in November and December, there was such general discouragement with the TEP, particularly with the scarcity of ward store supplies, that any therapy aide's opinion to the contrary would have been regarded by both ward staff and professionals as out of contact with reality.

At the level of professional staff, no cohesive project group was developed which might have exerted normative pulls in support of or against the program. Thus, no feeling of group morale provided incentives for the professional staff to work together to solve problems, while group norms among therapy aides were at best neutral toward the program. Certainly, there was little attempt in the planning for implementation of the program to mobilize a group dynamic among ward staff to work together to carry out the program.

In summary of the findings on intermediate-level processes, this section has shown that some positive features at this level supported the implementation of some parts of the TEP but that other components contributed to its overall lack of success. The positive supports focused on the early incorporation of token distribution and redemption routines into the standard procedures of the ward; the technical requirements of this part of the program were specified in sufficient detail by the initial plans to be compatible with staff orientations and ward routines. Other standard operating procedures, particularly those of the center as a whole, tended to add obstacles to the path of the TEP, while lack of supportive supervisory expectations, lack of technical plans for individual contributions from therapy aides, the absence of strong informal communication links to an expert source of technical advice on the program, and probably group norms inhibiting on-ward commitment to the program all served to undermine any problem-solving efforts which might further implementation of the remaining aspects of the TEP.

INDIVIDUAL-LEVEL VARIABLES

Since there was no individual measure of program implementation in this setting, little can be said about the possible relationship between individual differences and variable degrees of implementation by separate staff members. Similarly, it is impossible to separate the relative influences of individual- and intermediate-level components when no quantitative data are available and both types of influence are confounded within a program in a single setting. Nevertheless, some possible effects of individual level variables on the TEP will be suggested.

BEHAVIORAL SKILLS

As described above, some aspects of the TEP required individual contributions from therapy aides and proposed changed interaction patterns between patients and ward staff. It is doubtful that the in-service training provided was sufficient to overcome the limited educational backgrounds of the therapy aides. Four of the five interviewed had completed high school, while the other therapy aide had finished tenth grade. Only one of the five had taken any college courses, including one psychology course. Further, their average length of service at the Psychiatric Center was 12.5 years, so they would have been well socialized into the prevailing psychiatric treatment model. Within that model, the physician or outside program staff provided the therapy while the ward staff emphasized daily care and general supervision. Thus, neither their educational background nor their previous extensive work experience provided the behavioral skills that the ward staff would need to fully implement this program.

The lack of necessary behavioral skills was acknowledged by the psychologists, who hoped to build up the skills gradually in the process of joint treatment planning between psychologists and therapy aides. But this process itself was planned to be triggered on the initiative of the therapy aides, an action which assumed that therapy aides would not be intimidated by the status differences between themselves and psychologists. Then, when time pressures during summer vacations made joint planning difficult to arrange and psychologists lost credibility by not including the psychotic symptoms necessary for the plans to be approved by the Utilization Review Committee, the joint planning process broke down. Further, psychologists were not present on the ward often enough to model the desired positive modes of patient-staff interaction. Consequently, the inadequate behavioral skills of ward staff were not gradually shaped into those necessary to run the token economy. That therapy aides also felt this behavioral lack was shown by their nearly unanimous statements of need for more training during the interviews conducted in November and December.

INCENTIVE STRUCTURE

No institutional incentive structure was present to reward extra efforts by staff on behalf of the TEP. Because the Psychiatric Center was part of the state mental health system, its pay levels and promotional opportunities were controlled by civil service regulations. Several staff mentioned the lack of positive incentives for staff to persist with a new program, and even possible severe costs if a new effort with a patient backfired:

> The staff has no reward for carrying out programs. They were excited about starting the "levels" system for different types of patients, but when problems in it arose, staff enthusiasm fell through.

> If staff members try to tell some patients what to do, the patient may have an outburst. The job description of therapy aide doesn't include getting hit with a chair!

Several administrators, when asked what incentives staff members had to exert extra efforts for a new program, stated that no institutional means of incentives would be permitted but that therapy aides would have to be motivated by seeing the results in the patients. In the same interviews, however, these administrators acknowledged that progress with these long-term patients was likely to be slow and difficult. Therefore, depending on internal satisfaction from the results of their efforts would not seem sufficient to motivate changes in therapy aides' job behavior.

On the other hand, the distinction discussed in Chapter 2 between "jobholders" and "career builders" may provide a useful analysis of worker motivation in this situation. For both therapy aides and professional staff, years of working within a ponderous organization unresponsive to their efforts seem to have produced a predominant "jobholding" orientation. For example, although therapy aides were given no choice about working on this ward, most were not dissatisfied to work with these patients; they regarded it as just another job assignment that might or might not improve the patients. Even the professionals, most of whom had been at the center ten years or more, had a jaundiced view of the possibility of this program succeeding when others had failed. "The pathology of the organization will do it in," predicted one professional in late October. Without any one professional having enough power to directly manage the program, the slim chances for informal efforts to succeed would provide little incentive for the professionals to adopt other than a "jobholder" orientation. Perhaps only a fresh, career-building professional without years of negative experiences in the organization could have exerted the detailed management necessary to bring the pieces of the TEP together; such an individual was the catalyst for the adoption of the program but was lost before the program was implemented.

COGNITIVE SUPPORTS

Expressed beliefs about the concept of a token economy were surprisingly positive, given the degree of problems and level of frustration with the program apparent in the interviews. Most professional staff stated that it is an appropriate program for the type of patients on this ward, although on-ward staff also distinguished some patients that were either able to exploit the token system or too withdrawn from any human contact to benefit from it. Four out of five therapy aides believed it had helped change some patients' behaviors, although at least two of these four were very discouraged with the program by the time of the interviews. Several staff members mentioned that they had seen a similar program work elsewhere or had read about its success.

The expressed belief in the program might have been reflecting a perceived social desirability effect toward the interviewer or reluctance to counter professional opinions on the value of a token economy, although most respondants did not seem to hesitate in criticizing specific parts of the program. In addition, when asked how their co-workers felt about the TEP, therapy aides replied less positively, as was discussed in the section on work group norms. It appears that many ward staff were in favor of the program as an abstract concept but believed a number of the patients were inappropriate for it and/or that the lack of supplies and other organizational problems prevented its implementation in this setting. Further, one key person, the ward head nurse, was much more ambivalent in her beliefs about the program, which may have further reinforced a general group norm that extra efforts on the program were useless. The generally favorable cognitive beliefs toward this program were not sufficient to overcome the negatively perceived practical realities or to generate the necessary implementation behaviors.

In conclusion, individual-level variables were generally consistent with the patterns suggested by analysis of other levels. Some favorable elements, such as widespread belief in the overall appropriateness of the program, were not strong enough to overcome the lack of necessary behavioral skills and the scarcity of individual incentives to exert efforts beyond the duties formally required for one's job. While individual skills and motivations probably played a role in the demise of this program, the individual characteristics, within the time span studied here, were inseparable from the operation of organizational processes.

CONCLUSIONS

This analysis of the introduction of a token economy program in a Psychiatric Center has shown that the proposed implementation model can be usefully applied to organizational settings other than the one for which it was developed. Even though information about the development of the TEP was limited to qualitative analysis of interviews with a variety of organizational participants, the use of the model has illuminated the complexity of the implementation process. Nearly all of the components at the three levels of analysis had influential effects in this case study, even though more exact estimates of differential weights for the components are impossible to specify with this type of evidence.

Some indications of influences among the various components can also be suggested. The lack of control processes to coordinate the separate disciplines that made up the treatment team was especially debilitating to the program, for direct lines of influence from this component to many of the intermediate- and micro-level components are apparent. The ambiguous control structure left direct supervisory expectations for the ward staff ambivalent and helped to prevent the adoption of new procedures for day-to-day ward routines that were necessary for the TEP. The blurred authority structure also undermined incentives, particularly of the professional staff, to commit time and energy to the program. Then the flow of informal communications waned, which might have tapped technical advice to help solve problems, because each discipline felt the others were primarily jockeying for power positions rather than focusing their energies on the future of the program. The problems of control processes also contributed to the failure to implement the individualized treatment planning process, which in turn hindered the development of therapy aides' behavioral skills.

Second, resource problems constantly threatened the program. Particularly the scarcity of supplies for the ward store was a gap that needed to be bridged before other efforts were likely to be successful. Without effective back-up reinforcers, additional on-ward changes or incorporation of the use of tokens into individual treatment plans were not likely to bring about changes in patient behaviors. The lack of adequate store supplies also provided a cognitive justification for inaction: Why try to change things if there is little probability that the attempt will be successful? In addition, early changes in personnel holding several staff positions removed valuable staff resources at a crucial time in the program which might have provided substantially different behavioral skills and personal motivations in these key positions had they not occurred.

While other influences from the regulating environment and centerwide operating procedures could be suggested, the essential point is that these organizational processes are again seen to operate as a system. In order to change any one aspect of the system, attention must be directed to other elements which benefit from the previous state of affairs, which must be altered to be compatible with the desired changes or which are present at inadequate levels to support other processes within a new system. As this case study has shown, a gradual sliding apart of organizational elements that must work together to implement a new program is sufficient to undermine the chances for successful implementation.

In an insightful analysis of a failed attempt to change the bureaucratic structure of the U.S. State Department, Warwick (1975) emphasized that elements in both the internal and external environments of a bureaucracy place pressures on daily operations to continue in previously known and desired patterns. Although strong new leadership may try to disturb old structures, shown by Warwick's analysis of drastic cuts in hierarchical levels and degree of centralization, the prevailing pressures tend to regenerate the old patterns once the disturbing force is removed.

A similar regeneration of prevailing institutional patterns took place at the Psychiatric Center after the sudden changes which accompanied the introduction of the token economy. Although by official decision this new program was adopted and some parts of it were incorporated into ward routines, when strong leadership was removed, the program drifted back toward prevailing institutional patterns.

In the strongly flowing stream of organizational events, a new program can attempt to set its own course only with a determined helmsman to steer around rocky obstacles and keep the crew working toward the program's objectives rather than succumbing to the flow of the stream. Even so, the stream may frequently be too strong for a particular program to navigate; without changing the characteristics of at least part of the stream or removing some institutional obstacles, the program may founder.

6

Implications for Practice

The social system perspective applied to these studies of implementation has emphasized the interconnectedness of organizational processes. Similarly, analysts of ecological systems have noted the side effects that accompany nearly every change in a biological community and have concluded that "we can never do merely one thing" (Hardin, 1969). While this aphorism was intended to apply to the outcomes of an intervention, for social systems it is an apt conclusion about the processes of intervention as well. In organizations, we can never *do* merely one thing. In order to implement a new program that requires changes in some aspects of the ongoing organizational system, other processes within the system must be modified to be compatible. Activities occurring at all three levels of organizational life—the macro level of the organization as a whole, the intermediate level of work unit processes, and the individual level of the front-line implementors—can influence the success or failure of an innovation introduced into any level of the system.

The therapeutic programs analyzed here were introduced into the Developmental Center and the Psychiatric Center by a similar sequence of events. In each case, there was a decision by high-level administrators within the organization to undertake the program, but these decision-making processes did not include input from the ultimate users, the therapy aides. In both cases, the impetus for the adoptions came from psychologists, who were outside the major authority hierarchies. In both cases, training was provided for the therapy aides on the background and procedures for each program, but the training was not continued. Nor were there problem-solving sessions on a regular basis. In both organizations, high-level administrators appeared to believe that these processes were sufficient to obtain implementation of the new therapeutic programs into the daily activities in which therapy aides interacted with residents. Thus, in neither organization were procedures developed to integrate the programs into the total system of components that constitutes a complex organization.

This sequence of events seems to be fairly typical of the way innovations are introduced into many organizations. Whatever planning and analyses are done usually precede the decision to adopt the program and focus on the substance of the innovation in connection with the perceived needs of the organization and its clients. Training is then provided to familiarize the implementors with the rationale and procedures for the new program; varying degrees of "hands-on" experience with the innovation are incorporated into the training process. Typically, it is then expected that the implementing staff will start using the innovation, without much attention to whether it is compatible with their other duties or their own job expectations, whether adequate resources are provided, whether supervisory structures support the use of the innovation, and so forth. In short, innovations are often introduced without adequate attention to the organizational context of implementation.

In such a situation, the forces which supported and maintained the previously operating system are still present and are likely to create pressures against implementation of an innovation requiring substantial changes. These are the regenerative forces analyzed in some detail in Warwick's study (1975) of a failed attempt to change organizational structure in the State

Department. In that case, environmental pressures, such as the interests of congressmen whose continuing support was necessary for the overall conduct of the department, internal standard operating procedures for the department as a whole, and the expectations of individual staff members for career progression all coalesced to defeat an attempt to decentralize authority and reduce the number of hierarchial layers within one branch of the department. When the initial pressure behind the structural change was reduced by the resignation of the high-level administrator who had initiated the change, these regenerative forces gradually undermined the extent of change.

Similarly, the introduction of an innovative program into any organization can easily be undermined by the failure to create a congruent system of processes to support the program. Adequate planning before the decision to adopt and good training procedures for the staff education are both likely to be *necessary* for an innovation to produce an intended result. But, as this research has shown, they are not *sufficient* to ensure implementation of the innovation into daily routines or to secure institutionalization of the program within the organization after the force pushing for adoption, such as a key staff member, leaves the organization.

This monograph has addressed the problem of implementation by first developing an analytical framework of organizational processes that are likely to affect implementation. The framework was then applied to field studies of two mental health organizations, both undertaking new programs with behavioral psychology emphases: the Goal Planning system at the Developmental Center and a Token Economy Program at the Psychiatric Center. In both studies, a detailed examination of the development of the program revealed several interlocking explanations for the differential levels of implementation found. Intensive interviews with staff from all levels of both centers were examined qualitatively for information about the macro-level processes. In the Developmental Center, sufficient staff were available to permit quantitative analysis, using multiple regression methods, of the relative influence of intermediate- and individual-level components on the number of Goal Plans written by individual staff members. Both qualitative and quantitative methods have been useful in this investigation to illuminate various facets of the total implementation process.

SUMMARY OF FINDINGS AT
THE PSYCHIATRIC CENTER

In the study of the introduction of a Token Economy within one ward of the Psychiatric Center, interviews with more than 20 staff members in diverse roles revealed that efforts to implement the economy never included more than a minimal number of the intended changes in ward-level procedures. The absence of coordinating control processes to integrate ward procedures which were derived from very different theoretical bases—specifically a conflict in procedures advocated by nurses and psychologists—was found to be a primary explanation for the failure of its implementation. Another prime hindrance to full implementation was the resource problem centering on the scarcity of supplies to serve as back-up reinforcers in the ward store. In addition, pressures on administrators to meet externally set standards for accreditation pulled their time and attention away from constructing a new management system for the ward.

These macro-level influences undermining implementation at the Psychiatric Center were reflected by on-ward supervisory expectations which did not include the tasks for enacting the Token Economy as part of the normal job requirements for therapy aides. While some changes in ward routines were accomplished which got the Token Economy started, other needed changes in procedures, such as incorporating the tokens into individual treatment plans, were unsuccessful. Therefore, initial individual-level acceptance of the idea behind this program was not enough to overcome the numerous organizational factors hindering its implementation. After the departure of the one psychologist who pushed through the initiation of a Token Economy, no individual staff member had the will and the authority to find paths around the numerous obstacles to its full implementation.

SUMMARY OF FINDINGS AT
THE DEVELOPMENTAL CENTER

The larger-scale study at the Developmental Center permitted quantitative analysis of intermediate- and micro-level organizational processes. This analysis supported the central hypothesis implicit in the model: that differential degrees of program implementation are related to the whole set of both organizational and individual variables. Neither characteristics of the setting nor characteristics of the individuals alone enabled as adequate an explanation of implementation behaviors as both types of variables considered together.

At the intermediate level of the Developmental Center, supervisory expectations—those expressed by the charge nurses and those perceived by therapy aides—were independently related to the number of Goal Plans written, as were the presence of routines enabling predictability of on-unit procedures, a longer job time on the unit, and less frequent discussions with the peer group of co-workers. Individual background indicators of potential behavioral skills, such as educational level and number of courses in psychology, unexpectedly were not related to writing goal plans. However, other individual variables—specifically age, job satisfaction, a "professional" job orientation, and cognitive belief in and liking for therapeutic procedures—were predictors of Goal Plan writing.

Examination of the macro-level processes at the Developmental Center suggested many channels of influence from these higher-level processes which were likely to have influenced the intermediate and individual effects just summarized. The decision process by which Goal Planning was adopted did not include provision for additional staff on the residential units for carrying out the therapy detailed in Goal Plans, nor was there a plan for changing the supervisory structure to incorporate therapeutically oriented expectations for the therapy aides. The previous nursing care orientation was even reinforced by a strong regulatory environment emphasizing appropriate medical standards. Further, the laissez-faire control system for the program areas provided no mechanism for integrating the therapy received by each resident, and left the decision on the use of Goal Planning up to the judgment of each program area supervisor. In sum, pressures from the higher-level administrative actions were more likely to undermine than to support the full implementation of Goal Planning as a therapeutic process.

COMPARISON OF FINDINGS
ACROSS SETTINGS

A very basic difference between the two settings is the degree to which the programs were successfully implemented. At the Developmental Center, Goal Planned therapy was routinely carried out by some program areas and a substantial number of plans had been written by some unit therapy aides, albeit a minority. Thus, a low but continuous level of implementation had been achieved. In contrast, the Token Economy at the Psychiatric Center never had enough of its pieces together at the same time for it to be considered even partially implemented. Thus, in one case this analysis focused on differential degrees of implementation, while in the other the search was for reasons for failure.

In some respects the two settings were similar, because both the Developmental Center and the Psychiatric Center were part of the New York State Department of Mental Hygiene, with similar regulations to follow, the same civil service procedures for hiring staff, and comparable financial constraints limiting numbers of staff. On the other hand, their institutional histories and sizes were quite different, since the Psychiatric Center was much larger and over a hundred years old, while the Developmental Center was new and had only several hundred patients. A major result of the difference in institutional age was a differential length of time on the job for their staffs. The long job tenure of the Psychiatric Center staff in an unresponsive setting had produced a widespread reluctance to exert personal initiative, except by an employee who was new to the system.

MACRO-LEVEL PROCESSES

At the macro level, a comparison of processes reveals a number of similarities, but also some crucial differences. In both cases, decision processes were initiated by psychologists, who were outside the primary lines of authority. The resulting implementation problems tend to confirm the proposition stated in Chapter 2 that initiation of a program by those not in a direct line of supervision hinders implementation. In neither case was there participation by the ultimate users in the decision to adopt the program, which is likely to have depressed the extent of cognitive commitment by these individuals and was symptomatic of the lack of open communication for problem-solving. However, the more gradual introduction of Goal Planning contrasts sharply with the all-at-once decision to begin the Token Economy; gradual introduction may have enabled individuals to begin Goal Planning at the Developmental Center on a trial basis.

Examination of control processes in both cases revealed a centralized initial decision followed by a lack of involvement by central administrators in the detailed processes of implementation. Further, in both institutions, staff members were accustomed to strong directives from central administrators for carrying out policies or procedures that had priority with the administration. Thus, the laissez-faire management of these innovative programs may have signaled to lower-level staff that solving implementation problems was not a strong administrative expectation. These findings support the hypothesis developed in Chapter 2 that implementation will be hindered if central administrators do not strongly and actively support the innovation. The strategies used to secure implementation, which in both centers depended primarily on extra initiative to be exerted by individual staff members, also were not consistent with their prevalent control processes emphasizing hierarchical authority, thus supporting the consistency of control proposition derived in Chapter 2. The laissez-faire management was seen as particularly debilitating to the Token Economy, both because its technical requirements demanded a greater degree of coordination among the contributions of separate disciplines and because the disciplines which were supposed to cooperate within a treatment team had a prior history of jurisdictional conflicts.

Scarcity of resources, the third macro-level component in the implementation framework, was felt to be a hindrance to the implementation of both programs. In both situations, therapy aides believed that the number of staff positions was too small to carry out the on-ward therapy called for by the innovations. No provision had been planned at the time of adoption for the additional staff time Goal Planned therapy or a Token Economy would require. Further, the intermittent supply of back-up reinforcers for patients was a substantial problem for the Token Economy, which was likely to have a depressing effect both on patient motivation toward changed behavior and on staff morale toward continued attempts to implement other parts of the program.

To what extent the resource problems were realistically perceived barriers actually preventing implementation as opposed to convenient justifications for staff inaction is difficult to distinguish. Certainly staff who were not accustomed to exercising initiative for solving administrative problems could be expected to assume it was not their responsibility to solve these resource problems. On the other hand, resources such as staff positions and support funds are nearly always in short supply; staff who defer implementing actions until resource problems are solved are very likely to defeat the program altogether. Resolution of the possible causal effects of scarce resources would require experimental intervention to increase the level of resources or to change the level of staff action toward implementation in order to determine the causal ordering of these variables.

Pressures from external regulatory agencies are likely to have been one factor supporting the decisions to adopt both of these programs. But other external influences were primarily negative: Quality review of records, external inspections, the multiplicity of records, and ambiguous standards about patients' civil rights all tended to pull administrators' attention toward meeting externally set regulations and away from solving internal management problems. Lower-level staff often became frustrated with a lack of administrative support for their efforts with patients, as supervisors were perceived to place more emphasis on what was in the records than on what treatment was provided to patients. This in turn led to a compliance-with-rules orientation among lower-level staff which contradicted the problem-solving initiative needed for the new programs.

INTERMEDIATE-LEVEL COMPONENTS

At the intermediate level, characteristics of the immediate work settings were shown to have strong influence. As predicted from the review of previous literature, when the new program was derived from sources outside the immediate supervisor's background, supervisory cognitive orientations sometimes conflicted with the theoretical orientations of the new program and undermined implementation by lower-level staff. In these mental health centers, first-line supervisors were nurses whose training emphasized efficiency in patient care as well as therapeutic interventions. The data from the Developmental Center showed substantial gaps between therapy aides and nurses in their perceptions of the nurses' expectations for therapy, thus revealing problems in the communication of role expectations to therapy aides. Supervisory expectations for therapy, both actual and as perceived by therapy aides, were shown by the regression analysis to be predictors of Goal Planning, while the nonsupportive expectations of several nurses at the Psychiatric Center were also likely to have undermined the Token Economy there.

The presence of predictable work routines compatible with the innovations was found to be positively related to their implementation, particularly with the quantitative data from the Developmental Center. Further, within those parts of each setting in which the new program duties were *not* simply added to the existing set of duties—such as in specific program areas at the Developmental Center and for distribution of tokens to patients for small jobs previously done by staff—implementation success was much higher, thus supporting the hypothesis raised in Chapter 2. When a part of the innovation was perceived as adding additional work to an existing job role (for example, when therapy aides were asked to keep records of tokens distributed, special education teachers in the Developmental Center were to write Goal Plans in addition to daily lesson plans, or therapy aides in both centers had to conduct individual therapy with patients), the new job duties were resisted, usually successfully.

Both centers had introductory training sessions focusing on information transmittal about the new programs, but in neither case was this training sufficient in itself to bring about full implementation. The strategy of training therapy aides as individuals to implement the program was somewhat more successful with Goal Planning, because a low level of their use could be achieved by individual therapy aides who were highly motivated. In contrast, the implementation of most parts of the Token Economy required coordinated efforts from various types of staff, particularly therapy aides, nurses, psychologists, and psychiatrists. In this case, the training sessions were not designed to foster the coordination of team efforts that would be necessary to implement the economy. In neither center were there later problem-solving sessions to follow up on the initial training or to continue to teach staff members the roles and procedures required by the innovations. These observations support the hypothesis derived in Chapter 2, that the extent and types of training should be congruent with the technical requirements of the innovation. Specifically, when a new program is not fully specified in advance but requires details to be worked out by the implementors, it is likely that information-oriented training alone will not be adequate to bring about full implementation.

Communication patterns did not have as strong an influence in these settings as had been expected, for neither the extent of contact with the source of the innovation (the psychologists) nor the flow of communication between unit staff and program areas helped to predict the extent of Goal Planning at the Developmental Center. At the Psychiatric Center, communication between therapy aides and psychologists and between members of separate disciplines was at such a low level that the effect on a new program was bound to be negative. Further, levels of upward communication within hierarchical channels seemed to be low in both centers, since there was no participation by the direct implementors—the therapy aides—in the decisions to undertake these programs. Numerous staff members interviewed mentioned difficulty in getting higher-level administrators to understand the problems they were having with implementation.

The failure of regression coefficients to show influence for communication variables may have resulted from a fairly uniform dampening effect of blocked communication channels, rather than a lack of effect for communication. In this situation utilizing regression analysis for examining variations in implementation levels *among* the staff within one setting, the strength of a variable with a uniform depressing effect would not be revealed in the quantitative analysis. Comparison of several settings with different levels of communication would be necessary to estimate the strength of its association with implementation.

On the other hand, communication patterns within the work group on a ward or unit were found to have negative effects on further implementation in both settings. Using quantitative analysis of the Developmental Center and qualitative analysis of the Psychiatric Center, it was found that work group normative patterns were predominantly against the belief that the innovation would be beneficial to patients. Consistent with this belief pattern, the work groups in general did not actively support most efforts of their members to implement these programs, although they did not actively undermine individual efforts either.

INDIVIDUAL-LEVEL COMPONENTS

Some individual-level variables were found to have substantial effects on Goal Planning, but at the Psychiatric Center the available data were inadequate to separate individual influences from the effects of the setting. Surprisingly, hypotheses that higher levels of education and more background in psychology would facilitate individual implementation were not supported by data from the Developmental Center. Further, the significant effect for age there was negative, rather than the expected positive effect, which would reflect greater experience and therefore greater behavioral skill. It was widely believed by professional staff at the Psychiatric Center that therapy aides lacked the technical skills required for some parts of the Token Economy, particularly for writing individual therapy plans. This lack probably contributed to the program's demise when the behavioral skills were not developed as intended through a treatment planning process incorporating joint planning by therapy aides and psychologists.

The failure of measures of behavioral skills to be related to Goal Planning at the Developmental Center may result from the lack of externally provided incentives for individual performance. In these civil service positions, neither rate of pay nor likelihood of promotion was derived from performance in delivering therapeutic programs. Further, few social rewards, such as supervisor approval or esteem from co-workers, were likely to derive from extra effort spent on Goal Planning. However, several measures of internally felt incentives, such as overall job satisfaction and a "professional orientation" indicated by relevant outside reading, were found to be related to Goal Planning at the Developmental Center.

It is likely that most workers in both locations, even some professionals, were primarily "jobholders," oriented toward doing their job as expected by the environments they were in, rather than "career builders" seeking professional advancement through individual accomplishment. If so, as hypothesized in Chapter 2, their job orientations would be incompatible with the technical status of these innovations, which required implementors to create the specific procedures for application.

The final set of variables at the individual level, cognitive support from individual beliefs, attitudes, and felt needs was shown to have independent influence on Goal Planning at the Developmental Center. Measurements of liking for therapy and a positive attitude toward the potential effectiveness of Goal Planning for residents' development were each found to have a substantive effect within regression predictions of the number of Goal Plans written. At the Psychiatric Center, not enough therapy aides worked within the only Token Economy ward to enable quantitative analysis. However, the predominant belief seemed to be one of ambivalence: Most staff stated they liked the idea of a Token Economy in general but had doubts whether it was appropriate for several specific residents on the ward, or did not feel a personal challenge from working on it. In sum, individual cognitions appeared to have an influence on implementation in both centers, but this influence is not easily separated from the institutional context in which individuals worked.

Thus, in the study which involved sufficient numbers of staff for quantitative analysis to be undertaken at the individual level, regression weights for both individual and situational variables contributed to explaining the variability in level of Goal Planning. However, the individual-level variables which were influential here were those reflecting cognitive orientations and incentives for action, rather than measures of differential behavioral skills. Technical training by itself may have little impact toward changing behaviors if supportive cognitive and situational structures are not also present.

IMPLICATIONS FOR PROGRAM ADMINISTRATORS

The results of this study have a number of implications for administrators attempting to increase the extent of program implementation. The framework itself, as developed in Chapter 2 and summarized in Table 2.2, can serve as a reference list of components to be considered while planning the installation of a new program. A systematic assessment of the help or hindrance presented by each component can alert the administrator to potential problems while there is still time to address them. As one administrator expressed it, "It's better to treat the little monkeys before they become big gorillas!"

This assessment could include use of available data (even collection of new data if resources for this are available), formal or informal consultation with affected staff members, or simply analysis of the likely status of each component based on the personal experience of the administrator within the organization. The essential element is that the organizational changes required for implementation be given at least the same administrative attention as is devoted to the needs assessment, review of alternative programs, or other planning strategies governing the choice of the content of the program. As this research has shown, implementation requires more than just deciding to adopt a program, more than just providing training to the staff members who will be the program deliverers.

IMPLICATIONS FOR THE
DECISION-TO-ADOPT STAGE

Administrative assessment should continue during each stage of the implementation process. During the decision-to-adopt stage, influences from the macro-level components are likely to be most prominent. Supporters, opponents, and potential beneficiaries in the environment may be jockeying for influence over the program decision as well as for an advantageous future position vis-à-vis whatever program is adopted. The impact of the anticipated program for meeting regulatory requirements and its potential for attracting new funds or being a financial drain are likely to be major concerns of top-level administrators.

Amid these necessarily political pressures surrounding the decision-making processes, it has been easy for program managers to overlook the internal organizational components which will influence implementation of the program. A feasibility assessment during the decision-to-adopt processes could reveal the extent and types of internal changes likely to be necessary to bring about organizational congruence with the technical requirements of the innovation. What changes in standard operating routines will be needed? Will first-line supervisors view the innovation as a challenge, a routine change, or perhaps a threat to their status or professional authority? What types of regular communication channels will be needed, and are these already established? Will the beliefs of individual staff members and the content of work group norms be likely to support or undermine the innovation? What is the current status of the behavioral skills that will be required for the innovation and what training will be needed? Consideration of these and other questions suggested by the framework during the decision-to-adopt deliberations should contribute a realistic assessment of the probabilities for implementation. Differential assessment of the implementation likelihood for various programs being considered could even be entered into the decision regarding the choice of program.

ASSEMBLING RESOURCES

During the "assembling resources" stage, planning for implementation start-up will need to be concrete, specific, and realistic. Decisions governing the scope of the initial implementation will determine which staff members will be involved and from what locations. If staff are to be hired or reassigned, especially staff for the supervisory level, their expertise with and favorability toward the technical features of the specific innovation should be as carefully evaluated as their general background credentials and experience relevant to the position. Training sessions should include both implementing staff and their supervisors, should be behaviorally focused on the new skills and understandings that implementors will need to use, and should be evaluated for their success in imparting these skills and understandings. Material resources of equipment and supplies must be chosen, ordered, and followed up to ensure availability. An information system to provide feedback on the progress and effects of implementation should be designed and implemented at the same time as the service program itself. Consideration of the staff time needed for planning, consultation, problem-solving, and so forth should be included as a resource essential for at least the first few months of implementation. In sum, this period of time devoted to assembling the resources necessary for an integrated implementation should increase the likelihood of an initially successful trial period that will, in turn, reinforce staff efforts to extend the program.

ROLE CHANGE

At the heart of the implementation sequence is the renegotiation of role relationships of staff members as the actual implementation begins. Role changes are likely to be required to develop mutually supportive reciprocal expectations that are congruent with the behaviors required for the new program. This process may involve explicit discussion of and agreement about various participants' responsibilities, or it might occur by implicit adjustment if open communication already provides mutual feedback.

The program manager's role in this process could include task analysis for specific jobs, to look for evidence of incompatibility of old tasks with the activities required for the innovation. New communication channels—working committees, regular memos, joint planning of teams of staff members, feedback from other organizational units, and so on—may need to be established on a formal basis initially, even if more informal operation might be more efficient eventually. If work group norms are incompatible with the roles required by the innovation, the program manager should be sensitive to the staff's basis for opposition: Is it a desire for some control over their work situation, a lack of belief in the theoretical rationale for the program, experience-based cynicism concerning the reality of long-term administrative support for the program, or another possibly reasonable basis for a lack of enthusiasm?

Closely related to the initial role change processes required for implementation are problem-solving efforts. Although problem-solving is portrayed as a separate stage in the diagram of implementation processes shown in Figure 2.1, in order to emphasize the contingencies of successful implementation, the time relationships of role change and problem-solving are likely to be highly overlapping rather than sequential. Responsibility for problem-solving efforts should be explicitly assigned so that needs for expert technical advice, additional training, and reassignment of staff or other resources can be recognized and addressed before minor problems become magnified into major blocks to continued efforts toward full implementation.

The program manager, or delegated problem solver, would be wise to undertake a systematic assessment of each of the components in the implementation framework a short while after initial implementation—perhaps two or three months—to diagnose the status of the organizational system at that point. How much change has already occurred? What program elements still remain to be fully implemented? What barriers to implementation are perceived by the program deliverers, by their supervisors, by intended beneficiaries, or by other informed observers other than those directly responsible for the program? Several days' time, or even longer for a complex program, spent collecting and digesting information about the progress of implementation in its organizational context could uncover, and suggest solutions to, problems that might otherwise jeopardize the fruitfulness of the entire program effort.

INSTITUTIONALIZATION

Finally, the new program procedures should be institutionalized into the everyday operations of the organization, so that the special resources for problem-solving or staff training are no longer necessary. Instead, support for an institutionalized program would come from the normal budgetary allocations, normal procedures for staff recruitment and training, and usual planning mechanisms. The program manager's role in the transition to institutionalization may be more difficult for the manager than for other staff members, for it involves giving up the special status of being responsible for an innovative program, thus allowing the program to "grow up" and "fend for itself in the organizational jungles." While this transition might best be accomplished in connection with the normal turnover of the incumbent in the program manager's role, the process should be prepared for by having other staff members take over program activities formerly performed or coordinated by the program manager. Much more depth of analysis about institutionalization processes is provided by Yin's intensive analysis of "routinization" (1979) in urban bureaucracies.

This sequence of administrative involvement in implementation processes is not suggested as a panacea to make implementation easy, for it is likely to remain a complex and convoluted interplay of organizational and interpersonal forces. This investigation has shown that implementation processes can be analyzed into components; administrative intervention to facilitate favorable interactions from this set of components could bring about improved implementation. Given the complexity and number of influences likely to impinge on the implementation of each local program, even extensive further research is not likely to develop a standard prescription for ensuring implementation success. The role of the program manager will remain a critical facilitator of the necessary organizational change. The program manager must orchestrate and conduct numerous players in the new composition that is program implementation.

7

Implications for Research

The studies of implementation presented here reinforce the topic of implementation as one amenable to systematic empirical research. These studies have shown that both qualitative case studies and quantitative assessments of implementation are feasible within the conceptual framework developed here. Both methodologies have contributed to understanding the complex processes of implementation described in this monograph. For future research, quantitative and qualitative approaches should not be considered mutually exclusive, nor should one or the other be chosen primarily on the basis of the researcher's training or preferred style. Both should be used whenever practical in a particular research situation: the qualitative description to add exploratory depth and time-based analysis of change processes, the quantitative measurements for precise hypothesis-checking, comparability of information collected across settings, and assessment of objectivity across observers. To investigate a topic as complex as implementation processes, both types of investigations will be needed, together or separately.

THE SOCIAL SYSTEM PERSPECTIVE

The results of this research effort document the usefulness of the multilevel social system perspective for analyzing program implementation. No single component or few components of the conceptual framework were found to be primary explanations for the extent of implementation in the situations studied. The implication of this finding is that future research investigating implementation should include consideration of the social system operating in the research setting, even if the researcher's primary interest is in utilizing one of the other six theoretical approaches described in Chapter 2. Since implementation is, by definition, an applied research problem, the extent of experimental control that can be achieved within laboratory settings is usually not possible for implementation studies. Therefore, the researcher cannot *assume* that other conditions are equal or that differences between settings are randomly distributed; these differences must be examined, measured if possible, and included within the analytic discussion, even if the researcher's substantive interest is limited to the influences operating within one part of the social system. A similar emphasis on the social system surrounding the phenomenon of interest has recently been promulgated by Bronfenbrenner's (1979) ecological approach to research in applied child development. The emphasis of this approach is that the complexities of research on applied topics cannot be alleviated by ignoring the difficulties. Facing the complexities of the real world, including them in research designs, developing empirically based evidence for distinguishing major from minor influences, while accumulating the results of several individual studies is the sequence of steps which, over time, may foster simplification of the research or reveal implementation phenomena to be inherently complex.

On the other hand, the logic behind this position should not be carried to the extreme of suggesting that implementation processes are so complex that no rigorous empirical research is possible. One might posit a continuum of theoretical explanation from a single causal factor theory (y is "nothing but" x), through explanations encompassing several causal factors (y is a function of x_1, x_2, x_3, and x_4), to an extreme position that the necessary explanation is so complex that it is unknowable (however many X's are included in explanation of y, there is always "something else" that should have been included).[1] The position being advocated here is that implementation processes can be investigated with a finite number of explanatory variables, but that an adequately complex picture of the organizational system which fosters or hinders implementation will require at least the variables included as components of the framework developed here.

This framework was constructed to include the major explanatory factors suggested by the previous literature. The intention was to incorporate indicators of all major "causes" of implementation success or failure within one analytical approach. Over time, the use of the framework will reveal whether some components are never found to be major sources of implementation outcomes, and thus could be dropped from the framework, or whether there are additional major components which ought to be included.

As additional studies of implementation accumulate, it is expected that the particular components of the framework found to be most influential in a particular setting will differ from the specific components influencing another organization, even among organizations implementing the same innovative program or technology. This expectation flows from the inevitable differences among organizations before adopting the innovation—differences in structure, history, ongoing processes, personality characteristics of influential staff members, and environmental interests influencing events. In addition, variations in the impact of specific components will derive from the events occurring during the initial phases of the implementation, such as the decision processes, training mechanisms, and other contingencies which influence how the program or innovation gets started. But the thesis underlying the framework is that this set of components is sufficiently comprehensive to explain a wide variety of implementation situations.

Of course, the evidence presented in Chapters 4 and 5 is not nearly adequate to support this sweeping generalization. Research using a much wider range of innovations in a much larger and more generalizable sample of organizations would be needed to provide an adequate test of the framework. Further evidence could also be provided by the systematic comparison of case studies documenting specific program implementation attempts, if the studies incorporated enough components of the framework for legitimate comparison. The usefulness of the approach would be further validated by intervention planning which systematically considered each component in relation to the likely barriers or facilitators in a particular situation. Does such systematic diagnosis of problems facing an implementation attempt suggest ways of overcoming or reducing barriers, thus increasing the extent of implementation? From a combination of evidence from such varied sources, the generalizability and utility of the framework could be judged over time.

MEASUREMENT PROBLEMS

Within this diverse research agenda, measurement of both dependent and independent variables will remain problematic. In order for research results to be cumulative, it is essential that measurement of variables be comparable across settings. Yet, in order for measurements to be meaningful within the particular setting, past practice has been to construct measuring instruments specifically applicable to each study. This was, of course, the method used within the studies reported here, as well as by most previous implementation research (for example, Berman and McLaughlin, 1974; Beyer and Trice, 1978; Yin, 1979). It is likely that this measurement dilemma will continue to plague implementation research for some time; the only ameliorating suggestion is for researchers to pay serious attention to the instruments used by their predecessors in order to use them and build upon them. If no previous instrument can be used for a particular research effort, the investigator should attempt to construct new instruments with known comparability to prior ones.

Comparability of dependent variables might be improved by recognizing the multidimensional nature of the construct "implementation." Implementation will inevitably involve multiple behavioral and organizational changes needed to put into effect the program or technology, which itself incorporates multiple or unspecified component parts. Clear specification by the researcher of which aspect or aspects of implementation are intended by a particular measure should help to differentiate separate dimensions of this construct as the number of investigations increases.

Future research on implementation should incorporate greater attention to the dimension of time, for implementation is a set of processes which occur over time. The major justification for research on implementation questions is understanding how these changes are initiated, executed, and maintained over time. For policy purposes, the rationale of implementation research is to increase the extent to which important social programs are implemented in real situations. For these reasons, research confined to cross-sectional data-collection methodologies will not be adequate for a full understanding of the topic. Cross-sectional data do not provide firm evidence of the changes which occurred in the past which created the set of interrelationships existing at the time data are collected. Further, inferences about what interventions or policies could successfully increase the extent of implementation are very risky from such cross-sectional data. Berman (1980) has analyzed this problem as the distinction between analysis of process and analysis of variation, which, he states, lead to different types of explanation. He advocates that both types of analysis be fostered for studies of educational change.

The restriction of data collection to a single time period, with reliance on staff members' recollections of earlier events, is a limitation of the research reported here. Yet integration of the quantitative multiple regression results with qualitative process analysis from the interview materials has provided a richer view of the organizational dynamics underlying the statistical results.

DESIGNS FOR FUTURE RESEARCH

A more comprehensive integration of process and variance analyses could be achieved in future research by data collection at several points over the course of change. Provision for continuous data collection would be even better, although more expensive. The most important time periods for collecting observations in an ideal research design would be as follows:

(1) During the decision-to-adopt process, firsthand information should be obtained on types of participants and their interests in having the program adopted. Baseline information should be collected on

the structure and processes of relevant organizational components at that point in time.

(2) Three to six months after initial implementation efforts are attempted by program deliverers, measurements should be obtained of the extent of implementation by that time and of the changes in procedures, structures, and processes which have been initiated in support of implementation.

(3) A second wave of such implementation process data would be collected six to twelve months later, depending on the institutional cycle (for example, the school year or annual review cycle) of the organization being studied.

(4) If institutionalization had not taken place by the "second wave" collection period, which is likely for complex changes or multiple-unit organizations, a third wave of data would be valuable during the third to fifth year of implementation, assuming that the target program had survived that long.

The longitudinal research design outlined above would, of course, be expensive to utilize even within a small sample of organizations. However, it would provide a much fuller data set enabling measurement of change over time not only in the dependent variables measuring extent of implementation, but also in the organizational components which are hypothesized to determine the extent of implementation. In other words, this design would permit rigorous, quantitative assessment of both process and variability in the same study. It would also provide a firmer empirical foundation for policy recommendations regarding program implementation than has been possible heretofore.

An alternative, but less rigorous, approach to future investigation of implementation processes would be for a local program administrator to adopt an explicitly action-oriented research strategy using the organizational framework developed here. Within this approach, the administrator would systematically analyze his or her own organization at the beginning of an implementation effort, to diagnose which organizational components would be likely to contribute to the change and which might present problems. Measurement of the components in relation to the anticipated change would utilize available data, perceptions of a number of organizational staff members, or even the administrator's own subjective assessment based upon personal experience within the setting. Using this diagnosis of strengths and problems facing implementation, the administrator would next design and carry out an intervention action strategy to increase the probability of successful implementation. The aim should be to increase the congruence between the program implementation activities and the ongoing organizational system. It would be extremely desirable for the administrator to obtain periodic feedback information on the extent to which implementation was occurring, as well as information about the utilization of the action strategies. After a reasonable period of time, the extent of both program implementation and outcome effectiveness should be measured as objectively as is feasible, to provide validating data for the outcomes of the change effort. The greater the extent to which this action-oriented strategy includes precise measurements over time, the more nearly it would approximate the longitudinal research design described previously. The difference here is that intervention into the ongoing organizational system is explicitly included. To the extent that the framework fosters sufficient understanding of that system to facilitate successful change strategies, the usefulness of the framework is thereby substantiated.

Two problems can be noted with this approach. One is that even insightful, accurate diagnosis of barriers and facilitators facing the change attempt might not suggest adequate strategies to remove, get around, or otherwise solve problems hindering implementation. Second, even if the administrator devised a detailed, creative action strategy to solve program implementation problems, he or she might not have the power, resources, or skill to implement the action strategy! In these cases, the answer may be that program implementation is not necessarily possible in all organizations, for all programs; it may be impossible to modify the organizational system sufficiently to permit implementation of an incongruent innovation.

This discussion of future research strategies for investigating problems of implementation has emphasized that a variety of approaches, designs, and data-collection methodologies could usefully further both implementation research and the application of this research to implementing programs in real organizations. A number of research difficulties, particularly in measuring some key variables, remain in need of methodological development. But the consistent theme of this discussion has been to stress the need for future investigations to encompass the organizational context of the change effort occurring.

Research perspectives are inadequate which include only a small part of that context, such as investigating only the beliefs of implementors, or only the extent of participation in decisions, or only the support of supervisors for an implementation effort. Each of these factors is indeed likely to be an important contributor to the extent of implementation; all are included in the framework of components developed in Chapter 2. Yet without inclusion of the other components in the research design, the investigator has no basis to judge their relative importance even to a specific situation. The body of research conducted within a variety of competing perspectives simply becomes diffuse and inconclusive, rather than accumulating evidence to provide a coherent set of findings.

Implementation researchers, utilizing their diverse perspectives, might be seen as similar to the six blind men describing an elephant, each of whom could collect observations only by feeling a different part of its anatomy. What if these six blind men tried to teach the elephant to do a new task? Without coordination and integration of their individual observations, they would have little way of knowing whether the beast was moving appropriately, nor could they signal the elephant positive feedback for changes in the desired directions. Similarly, without some knowledge of how the elephant functions as a biological system, they would be unable to estimate the animal's need for more or less food to supply energy for a different set of tasks. The analogy between a biological system and a social system is only partially appropriate and should not be carried too far. Nevertheless, this research has shown that the implementation of social programs requires an integrated framework to locate implementation analysis within its organizational context.

NOTE

1. I am grateful to Robin M. Williams, Jr. for the "nothing but" versus "something else" description of types of theory in social science.

APPENDIX A
SAMPLE OF GOAL PLAN FORM

DEPT. OF MENTAL HYGIENE DEVELOPMENTAL SERVICES GOAL PLANNING SYSTEM* GOAL PLAN	1. New X / MODIFY / UPDATE / CORRECT / DELETE	2. Resident / Client ID `2 1 0 7`	3. Goal Number `1 2 0 1`
		4. Problem / Deficit Number `D 1 0`	
		5. Name Henry Dickenson	

6. Problem / Deficit Domain `N 1 0 1 0 3`

7. Self help - Dressing - Pants

8. Problem / Deficit `[ ]`

9. " Henry doesn't know how to put on and fasten his pants

10. Document Number `[ ]`

11. Goal Domain `1 0 1 0 3`

12. Self-help - Dressing - Pants

13. Goal `[ ]`

14. " With pants placed in front of Henry, he will complete the task without assistance when told "Put on your pants." Criterion: 5 consecutive correct trials.

15. Document Number `[ ]`

16. Existing Program Number `G 1 0 1 0 7`

17. Present Behavior / Skill Level `[ ]`

18. Henry cannot perform the first step but will allow a staff member to guide his hands through the process.

19. Goal Rationale `[ ]`

20. Decrease dependence on other adults

21. Effective Date `0 4 0 1 7 5` Mo. Day Yr.

22. Milestone Date `0 4 1 5 7 5` Mo. Day Yr.

23. Target Date `0 6 0 1 7 5` Mo. Day Yr.

24. Type of Intervention & Discipline `1 1 0 0 1`

25. Self help skill training -- Unit/cottage staff

26. Intervention Plan / Method `[ ]`

27. gradually withdrawing physical assistance from last sequential step in the behavior chain to the first until the task is performed independently.

28. Document Number `[ ]`

29. Intervention Rationale `[ ]`

Has proven effective with residents at Henry's functioning level

30. _____

Phil Phillips
31. Program / Service Supervisor

Ron Riley
33. Program / Service Implementor II

Dan Thomas
32. Program / Service Implementor I

34. Program / Service Implementor III

	Monday	Tuesday	Wednesday	Thursday	Friday	Saturday	Sunday
35. Schedule	1	1	1	1	1	1	1
36. Time	0 6 3 0	0 6 3 0	0 6 3 0	0 6 3 0	0 6 3 0	0 7 3 0	0 7 3 0
37. Duration in Minutes	1 5	1 5	1 5	1 5	1 5	1 5	1 5

38. Minutes / Week `1 4 5` Hrs. Min.

39. Comment Dan Thomas on Monday through Friday
Ron Riley on weekends

209

*Developed by Nurhan Findikyan, Ph.D., Phillip H. Miller, M.A., and Terry M. Huff, M.A., Goal Planning for the Mentally Retarded Project, Tennessee Dept. of Mental Health and Mental Retardation, Supported by Region IV, SRS-DHEW HIP GRANT 51-P-20507-4-01.

**Include (a) name, (b) behavior, (c) condition, (d) baseline or criterion.

APPENDIX B

GOAL PLAN CODE SHEET

Goal Plan Code Sheet   Card # _____
                                                                       (1-3)

Unit # _____   Client # _____   Coder _____
   (4-5)   (6-8)   (9)

                           Unit or   Month

GP Written by _____   Program area _____   Written _____
       (10-12)   (13-14)   (15-18)

Other Implementers _____   _____   _____
                  (19-21) (22-24) (25-27)

Type of Goal _____   If "other", specify _____
     (28-29)   _____

Goal observable? _____
             (30)

Plan specific?   _____   (Code: 3 = yes, 2 = ?, 1 = no)
          (31)

Milestones: Total number of Milestones _____
                               (32)

1) Months after G P _____   Writer: _____
            (33)   (34-36)

    Content Code: _____   If "other", specify _____
         (37-38)

2) Months: _____   Writer: _____
      (39)   (40-42)

    Content Code: _____   "Other": _____
        (43-44)

3) Months: _____   Writer: _____
      (45)   (46-48)

    Content Code: _____   "Other": _____
        (49-50)

4) Months: _____   Writer: _____
      (51)   (52-54)

    Content Code: _____   "Other": _____
        (55-56)

5) Months: _____   Writer: _____
         (57)   (58-60)
       Content Code: _____   "Other": _____
         (61-62)

Overall Status of Plan at Present _____
               (63-64)

Problems:	Deficits:
1. _____	1. _____
2. _____	2. _____
3. _____	3. _____
4. _____	4. _____
5. _____	5. _____
6. _____	6. _____

INTRODUCTORY EXPLANATION
OF RESEARCH PROJECT

My name is _____ , and I am a graduate student at Cornell (SUNY-Binghamton) helping with this research project. The project focuses on the kinds of work people do, and how people feel about various aspects of their jobs. We are also interested in how different job roles relate to the introduction of a new development in mental health organizations, such as Goal Planning. The overall results, but not individual information, will be utilized by the Center as a Medical Care Evaluation Study for submission to Albany, so the study has been approved by the Research Committee. The major purpose is to examine and, hopefully, to improve the work situation here at the Developmental Center, by taking into account the views of Therapy Aides. The study is also part of Mary Ann Scheirer's doctoral dissertation in Social Psychology at Cornell.

I want to assure you that all individual data and anything you say during the interview are completely confidential. Only research staff not connected with the Developmental Center will ever see individual data, and even research staff will be working mainly with grouped data. Your participation is also completely voluntary both for the overall interview and any particular question, so just say so if you'd rather not answer any question. I expect the interview will take about an hour.

Of course, there are no "right" or "wrong" answers to the type of questions in this interview. We're just interested in your feelings about your job, and your point of view about Goal Planning. Do you have any questions about the research project before we begin the interview?

APPENDIX D

INTERVIEW SCHEDULE FOR THERAPY AIDES

INTERVIEW # _____   DATE _____

INTERVIEWER _____

1 _____   Introductory explanation of the research project.

2-4 _____   1. What is your job title now? _____

            And you work on what unit? _____

5 _____   And you work on what shift? _____

6-11 _____   2. Sex _____ Date of Birth _____

12-15 _____   3. How would you describe the actual work of your job here?

16 _____

17-18 _____

19 _____

20 _____

21-22 _____

23 _____

24 _____

25 _____   4. Do you know fairly well when you come in to work what you will be doing that day?

_____

30-31 _____   5. How long have you worked here at the Developmental Center?

_____

            (in months)

32 _____   6. Have you worked on your present unit the whole time? Y _____ N _____ If no, what other unit(s) have you worked on, for what periods of time? What shift was that?

33 _____

34-35 _____

36-37 _____

38 _____   7. What did you do before working here? (Give brief work history, if any, especially if any background in nursing or hospital work or mental health or research.)

39 _____

            8. What is your educational background?

            ____Less than high school graduation

            ____High school graduate (or high school equivalency)

40 _____   ___High school + non-college special course in business, nursing or other. (Specify): _____
    ___Some college. (Specify): _____
    ___College graduate. (Major?): _____

41-42 _____   ___Graduate work in? _____
    ___Graduate degree _____ In what field?

43 _____   9. (If any college) Have you ever taken any psychology courses?
    ___Y   ___N If yes, about how many?

44 _____

45 _____ 10. Do you ever do any reading about mental retardation problems, such as an article about a particular client's problem, or research results about behavioral methods, and so forth?
    ___Y   ___N If yes, what type of reading?
    About how often do you do this?

11. From the activities on this list (give Activities List) can you tell me which ones you spend a lot of time on in your job (ranked 4), which you spend a moderate amount of time on (ranked 3), which you do only a little (2), and which not at all (1)?

	ACTIVITY	Q-11	Q-12	Q-13	Q-14	Q-15
50-54	1) Cleaning					
55-59	2) Daily care					
60-64	3) Disciplining					
65-69	4) Nursing care					
70-74	5) Recreation within unit					
Card 2						
15-19	6) Recreation outside					
20-24	7) Responsibility for services					
25-29	8) Social skills training					
30-34	9) Staff supervision					
35-39	10) Teaching daily living skills					
40-44	11) Teaching communication					
45-49	12) Transporting clients					
50-54	13) Written work, therapy plans					
55-59	14) Written work, medical					
60-64	15) Physical therapy exercises					
65-69	16) Others?					

12. Now think about how *important* each activity is in *your* view of your major job responsibilities. Is the activity part of what you *should* be doing or not? Please rate each activity as a central responsibility of your job (=4), of some importance to your job (=3), of minor importance to your responsibilities (=2), or not really part of your major job duties (=1).

13. How about your likes and dislikes concerning these job activities. Are there any that you like a lot and want to do more often? (check).

14. Are there any that you dislike and would want to do less often, if other staff were available to do them? (check those mentioned).

15. What do you think are your immediate supervisor's views about which activities you should emphasize? ("Supervisor" is the charge nurse for the unit for each shift). For example, what things might you be reminded of if they don't get done? Please rate each activity as very important to your supervisor's expectations for your job (=4), somewhat important to your supervisor (=3), of minor importance to your supervisor (=2), or of no importance, your supervisor doesn't expect you to do this at all (=1).

16. Now I'd like to ask your reactions to several different aspects of your job, using these lists of adjectives and phrases (give Job Description Inventory for respondent to fill in.) For each word at the top of a column, such as WORK, PAY, SUPERVISOR and so forth, how descriptive of your feelings is each word or phrase beneath it? Just write Y for "yes" N for "no", and ? if you cannot decide.

Card 3

15 _____ 17. When interviewee has completed Job Description Inventory:
Overall, how satisfied with your job do you feel?
Would you say you are:

| Very Satisfied | Fairly Satisfied | Moderately Satisfied | Fairly Dissatisfied | Very Dissatisfied |

16 _____ 18. Do you ever ask your supervisor for advice or help in your work? About how often?

17 _____

18 _____ 19. What kinds of problems would you ask your supervisor about? Examples?

19 _____ 20. How about your co-workers? Do you ever ask them for advice or discuss problems about your work? How often?

20 _____ 21. Do there seem to be differences of opinion among the Therapy Aides on your unit on what to do about a problem? Can you give me an example of the different points of view?

_____

22. Thinking about your contacts with staff in various program areas how often would you say that you talk with staff in each area about client related problems? For example, about how often do you you talk with a *social worker* about progress or changes of a client?

	Once a day or more	Several times a week	About once a week	1 to 3 times per month	Less than once a month	Never
25 _____ Social Workers						
26 _____ Psychologists						
27 _____ Special Education Teachers						
28 _____ Children's Habilitation Staff						
29 _____ Occ. Therapy Staff						
30 _____ Physical Therapy Staff						
31_____ Speech & Hearing Staff						
32 _____ Voc. Rehabilitation Staff						
33 _____ Nurses not on your unit						
34 _____ Therapy Aides from other units						

23. (For those mentioned as once a week or more) What kind of problems do you discuss with _____?

_____

_____

Let's turn now to your ideas about the Goal Planning system.

40 _____ 24. What do you think of Goal Planning, in general?

41 _____

42 _____

43 _____ 25. Have your feelings about Goal Planning changed during the time
you have worked here? (When? How? Why?)

44 _____

45 _____

46 _____ 26. Did you have training for Goal Planning during your orientation
training period? ___Y ___ N

47-48 _____ 72. Can you recall how long this was? _____hours.

49-50 _____ 28. Have you had any additional training meetings since then? If yes,
what kind of training was this?

51 _____ 29. How would you rate the adequacy of the training sessions on
Goal Planning? Would you say they were:

___More than enough, (that they got boring)
___Just about the right amount
___Not enough training to understand the Goal Plans system
___Don't remember
___Other: _____

52 _____ 30. At the end of your training about Goal Planning, did you have a
clear idea of what you were expected to do to carry out this
method? If yes, can you describe briefly your understanding
about this? If no, what was unclear about it at the time?

53 _____

31. How about now, do you now have a clear idea of what you are
expected to do in connection with Goal Planning?
(Details as above)

54 _____

55 _____ 32. About how many Goal Plans have you written during the past year, say since September, 1976? _____._____

56 _____ 33. About how many others have you followed, or helped to implement, since September, 1976? _____

57 _____ 34. For what kinds of behaviors or problems do you use Goal Planning?

58 _____
59 _____
60 _____

61 _____

62 _____ 35. Are you doing therapy or teaching with clients that is not written up in Goal Plans? Examples? How often?

63 _____

36. Preliminary interviews for this study have brought up a number of issues that some Therapy Aides find to be problems or difficulties in their own attempts to implement Goal Planning. For each of the statements on this list, (give problem list to interviewee) can you indicate how much of a problem it has been for *you*? Do you feel it is a major difficulty in your attempts to do Goal Planning, (rate 3), a minor difficulty (2), or no problem at all for you (1)?

   65 _____ a) Not enough time to write Goal Plans.
   66 _____ b) Not enough time to carry out Goal Plans after they are written.
   67 _____ c) Knowing what is a good therapeutic intervention to teach a behavior or reduce a problem.
   68 _____ d) Finding the right wording to specify a treatment goal or activity.
   69 _____ e) The Goal Plan system is not flexible enough for the kinds of treatment needed by some clients.
   70 _____ f) Getting other staff on the unit to carry out the Goal Plan.
   71 _____ g) Having enough staff on the unit to carry out the Goal Plan.
   72 _____ h) Obtaining coordination among staff of various program areas for a unified approach to an intervention.

73 _____ i) Obtaining support from my supervisor for doing Goal Planned interventions.

74 _____ j) Obtaining suggestions and guidance from Psychologists.

75 _____ k) Delay in obtaining approval for a Goal Plan from the Psychologist or Resident Advisory Committee.

76 _____ l) Writing Goal Plans seems like useless paperwork since the treatment would be done anyway without it.

37. Are there any other problems or difficulties you can think of about Goal Planning, that you or other staff members have had?

Card 4

15 _____

16 _____ 38. The next question deals with *your* beliefs about the Goal Planning System. From this list of possible reasons for Goal Planning suggested by previous interviews, would you pick up to three items that best express your views on what are its major purposes?

17 _____

18 _____

19 _____ 39. From this same list, which of these purposes do you believe are actually being accomplished by Goal Planning on your unit now? Can you pick one to three items from this list?

20 _____

21 _____

		Q−40 Supervisor	Q−41 Psychologists	Q−42 Co-workers
_____	Very supportive and helpful			
_____	Supportive, but doesn't have enough time &/or knowledge about it to be very helpful			
_____	Doesn't help much, but doesn't hinder			
_____	Has opposed or otherwise hindered Goal Planning efforts. (Get details—When? Why?)			

40. What reaction do you feel you have received from your supervisor for your efforts toward Goal Planning?

41. What reaction do you feel you have received from the Psychology staff? (Use above responses)

42. What reaction have you received from your co-workers in your efforts toward Goal Planning? (Use responses above)

30 _____ 43. Are other staff members on your unit generally in favor of Goal Planning or not? What seems to be the group feeling on your unit about it?

_____

44. Finally, I have another short questionnaire I'd like you to fill out, about your feelings in this job. (Give Job Attitudes Questionnaire)

That's the end of the interview questions. I've been asking you a lot of questions—do you have any questions you'd like to ask me?

Thank you *very* much for participating in this study.

ACTIVITIES LIST

(List handed to interviewee for questions 11 to 15)

1. Cleaning or other maintenance of physical facilities.
2. Daily care of clients in feeding, dressing, toileting, etc.
3. Disciplining clients or correcting problem behaviors.
4. Nursing care, such as passing medications or caring for sick clients
5. Play/recreation activity with clients, within the unit.
6. Play/recreation activity with clients, outside the center, such as van rides or outside play.
7. Responsibility for clients' needs for new services, new clothing, etc.
8. Social skills training with clients.
9. Supervision of other staff, including scheduling.
10. Teaching activities of daily living to clients.
11. Teaching speech or communication skills to clients.
12. Transporting clients to programs or services.
13. Written work connected with planning therapy, including Goal Planning.
14. Written work on medical records.
15. Physical therapy exercises, as range of motion, or positioning.
16. Other?

REASONS FOR GOAL PLANNING

(List handed to interviewee for questions 38 and 39)

(a) By keeping careful records of client progress with Goal Planning, the therapist gets a stronger sense of accomplishment.

(b) Create formal records of treatment for legal purposes.

(c) Goal Plans stimulate more careful and specific planning by therapists, which leads to improved client capabilities.

(d) Goal planning is not useful at all.

(e) Provides security to therapy aides by having a Qualified Mental Health Professional review and approve treatment plans.

(f) The plan communicates to other staff members on the unit when cooperation with a client's therapy is needed.

(g) The plans help coordinate therapeutic activities among staff in various program areas.

(h) Written plans stimulate the therapist who wrote the plan to carry out the treatment consistently and conscientiously.

(i) Other?

References

Allison, Graham T. (1971) Essence of Decision: Explaining the Cuban Missile Crisis. Boston: Little, Brown.

Atthowe, J. M., Jr. and L. Krasner (1968) "Preliminary report on the application of contingent reinforcement procedures (token economy) on a 'chronic' psychiatric ward." Journal of Abnormal Psychology 73: 37-43.

Ayllon, T. and N. H. Azrin (1968) The Token Economy: A Motivational System for Therapy and Rehabilitation. New York: Appleton-Century-Crofts.

Baldridge, J. Victor and Robert A. Burnham (1975) "Organizational innovation: individual, organizational and environmental impacts." Administrative Science Quarterly 20: 165-76.

Banfield, Edward C. (1976) "Making a new federal program: model cities, 1964-68," pp. 183-218 in W. Williams and R. F. Elmore (eds.) Social Program Implementation. New York: Academic Press.

Bardach, Eugene (1977) The Implementation Game: What Happens After a Bill Becomes a Law. Cambridge: MIT Press.

Beckhard, Richard (1969) Organizational Development: Strategies and Models. Reading, MA: Addison-Wesley.

Bem, Daryl J. (1972) "Self-perception theory," pp. 1-62 in L. Berkowitz (ed.) Advances in Experiemental Social Psychology, Vol. 6. New York: Academic Press.

Berk, Bernard B. and Victor Goertzel (1975) "Selection versus role occupancy as determinants of role-related attitudes among psychiatric aides." Journal of Health & Social Behavior 16: 183-91.

Berman, Paul (1980a) "Thinking about programmed and adaptive implementation: matching strategies to situations," pp. 205-227 in D. Mann and H. Ingram (eds.) Why Policies Succeed and Fail. Beverly Hills, CA: Sage.

——— (1980b) "Toward an implementation paradigm of educational change." (unpublished)

——— (1978) "The study of macro- and micro-implementation." Public Policy 26: 157-184.

——— and Milbrey McLaughlin (1978) Federal Programs Supporting Educational Change, Vol. VIII: Implementing and Sustaining Innovations. Santa Monica, CA: Rand.

——— (1974) Federal Programs Supporting Educational Change, Vol. I: A Model of Educational Change. Santa Monica, CA: Rand.

Berman, Paul and Edward W. Pauly (1975) Federal Programs Supporting Educational Change, Vol. II: Factors Affecting Change Agent Projects. Santa Monica, CA: Rand.

Beyer, Janice M. and John M. Stevens (1976) "The routinization of change: implementation of policy in federal organizations." Prepared for the annual meeting of the American Sociological Association, New York, August 1976.

Beyer, Janice M. and Harrison M. Trice (1978) Implementating Change: Alcoholism Policies in Work Organizations. New York: Free Press.

――― (1977) "Organizational structure and the implementation of change within federal sector organizations." Prepared for the Academy of Management Annual Meeting, Kissimmee, Florida, August 14-17, 1977.

Blau, Peter M. (1963) The Dynamics of Bureaucracy: A Study of Interpersonal Relations in Two Government Agencies. Chicago: University of Chicago Press.

Bronfenbrenner, Urie (1979) The Ecology of Human Development: Experiments by Nature and Design. Cambridge, MA: Harvard University Press.

Bullock, Charles S. III (1980) "The Office for Civil Rights and implementation of desegregation programs in the public schools." Policy Studies Journal 8: 597-616.

Burns, Tom and G. M. Stalker (1961) The Management of Innovation. London: Tavistock.

Campeau, Peggie L. et al. (1979) Evaluation of Project Information Package Dissemination and Implementation: Final Report. Palo Alto, CA: American Institutes for Research and RMC Research Corp.

Chase, Gordon (1979) "Implementing a human services program: how hard will it be?" Public Policy 27: 385-435.

Coch, L. and J.R.P. French, Jr. (1948) "Overcoming resistance to change." Human Relations 1:512-533.

Cohen, Michael D. and James G. March (1974) Leadership and Ambiguity: The American College President. New York: McGraw-Hill.

Cole, Robert F. (1979) "Social reform frustrated by bureaucratic routine: Title XX in Massachusetts." Public Policy 27:273-299.

Corwin, Ronald G. (1972) "Strategies for organizational innovation: an empirical comparison." American Sociological Review 37:441-454.

Counte, Michael and John R. Kimberly (1974) "Organizational innovation in a professionally dominated system: responses of physicians to a new program in medical education." Journal of Health & Social Behavior 15:188-198.

Derthick, Martha (1976) "Washington: angry citizens and an ambitious plan" pp. 219-242 in W. Williams and R. F. Elmore (eds.) Social Program Implementation. New York: Academic Press.

Dornbush, Sanford M. (1976) "A theory of evaluation applied to schools." Prepared for the annual meeting of the Sociological Research Association, New York, September 1, 1976.

Elmore, Richard F. (1978) "Organizational models of social program implementation." Public Policy 26:185-228.

――― (1975) "Design of the Follow Through experiment," pp. 23-45 in Alice M. Rivlin and P. Michael Timpane (eds.) Planned Variation in Education: Should We Give Up or Try Harder? Washington, DC: Brookings.

Emrick, John and Susan M. Peterson (1978) A Synthesis of Findings across Five Recent Studies in Educational Dissemination and Change. San Francisco: Far West Laboratory for Educational Research and Development.

Eveland, J. D., Everett M. Rogers, and Constance Klepper (1977) The Innovation Process in Public Organizations. Ann Arbor: Department of Journalism, University of Michigan.

Fairweather, George W., David H. Sanders, Louis G. Tornatzky, and Robert N. Harris, Jr. (1974) Creating Change in Mental Health Organizations. Elmsford, NY: Pergamon.

Farrar, Eleanor, John E. DeSanctis, and David K. Cohen (1979) "Views from below: implementation research in education." Cambridge, MA: Huron Institute. (unpublished)

Findikyan, Nurhan, Terry Huff, and Phillip Miller (1975) "The generalized Goal Planning project." Presented at the Regional Workshop on Assessment Instruments and Systems, Tennessee Department of Mental Health, Knoxville, Tennessee, July 22, 1975.

Fishbein, Martin and Icek Ajzen (1975) Belief, Attitude, Intention and Behavior: An Introduction to Theory and Research. Reading, MA: Addison-Wesley.

Freedman, J. L. and S. C. Fraser (1966) "Compliance without pressure: the foot-in-the-door technique." Journal of Personality and Social Psychology 4:195-202.

Fullan, Michael (1972) "Overview of the innovative process and the user." Interchange 3 (2-3):1-46.

——— and Alan Pomfret (1977) "Research on curriculum and instruction implementation." Review of Educational Research 47:355-397.

Garfinkel, Harold (1967) "'Good' organizational reasons for 'bad' clinic records," pp. 186-207 in H. Garfinkel, Studies in Ethnomethodology. Englewood Cliffs, NJ: Prentice-Hall.

Gersten, Russell and Doug Carnine (1980) "Measuring implementation of the Direct Instruction Model in an urban school district: an observational approach." Presented at the annual meeting of the American Educational Research Association, Boston, April 1980.

Gilbert, John P., Richard J. Light, and Frederick Mosteller (1975) "Assessing social innovations: an empirical base for policy," pp. 39-193 in C. A. Bennett and A. A. Lunsdaine (eds.) Evaluation and Experiment. New York: Academic Press.

Gordon, G. and E. V. Morse (1975) "Evaluation research," pp. 339-361 in A. Inkeles (ed.) Annual Review of Sociology, Vol. 1. Palo Alto, CA: Annual Reviews.

Gouldner, Alvin W. (1954) Patterns of Industrial Bureaucracy. New York: Free Press.

Graen, George (1976) "Role-making processes within complex organizations," pp. 1201-1245 in Marvin D. Dunnette (ed.) Handbook of Industrial and Organizational Psychology. Chicago: Rand McNally.

Gramlich, Edward and Patricia Koshel (1975) Educational Performance Contracting: An Evaluation of an Experiment. Washington, DC: Brookings.

Greenblatt, Milton, Myron R. Sharaf, and Evelyn Stone (1971) Dynamics of Institutional Change: The Hospital in Transition. Pittsburgh: University of Pittsburgh Press.

Greenwood, Peter W., Dale Mann, and Milbrey W. McLaughlin (1975) Federal Programs Supporting Educational Change, Vol. III: The Process of Change. Santa Monica, CA: Rand.

Gross, Neal, Joseph B. Giacquinta, and Marilyn Bernstein (1971) Implementing Organizational Innovations: A Sociological Analysis of Planned Educational Change. New York: Basic Books.

Haga, William J., George Graen, and Fred Dansereau, Jr. (1974) "Professionalism and role making in a service organization: a longitudinal investigation." American Sociological Review 39:122-133.

Hage, Jerald and Michael Aiken (1970) Social Change in Complex Organizations. New York: Random House.

——— (1967) "Program change and organizational properties: a comparative analysis." American Journal of Sociology 72:503-519.

Hall, Gene E. and Susan F. Loucks (1977) "A developmental model for determining whether the treatment is actually implemented." American Educational Research Journal 14:263-276.

Hall, Gene E. and William L. Rutherford (1976) "Concerns of teachers about implementing team teaching." Educational Leadership 34:227-233.

Hall, Gene E., Archie George, and William Rutherford (1977) Measuring Stages of Concern about the Innovation. Austin: Research and Development Center for Teacher Education, University of Texas.

Hall, Richard H. (1972) Organizations: Structure and Process. Englewood Cliffs, NJ: Prentice-Hall.

Hardin, G. (1969) "The cybernetics of competition: a biologist's view of society," pp. 275-296 in P. Shepard and D. McKinley (eds.) The Subversive Science: Essays Toward an Ecology of Man. Boston, MA: Houghton Mifflin.

Hargrove, Erwin C. (1975) The Missing Link: The Study of Implementation of Social Policy. Washington, DC: Urban Institute.

Hasenfield, Yeheskel (1971) "Organizational dilemmas in innovating social services: the case of the community action centers." Journal of Health and Social Behavior 12:208-216.

Havelock, Ronald G. et al. (1970) A Guide to Innovation in Education. Ann Arbor: Institute for Social Research, University of Michigan.

Herriott, R. E. and N. Gross [eds.] (1979) The Dynamics of Planned Educational Change. Berkeley, CA: McCutchan.

Holland, Thomas P. (1973) "Organizational structure and institutional care." Journal of Health and Social Behavior 14:241-251.

Houts, Peter S. and Robert A. Scott (1975) Goal Planning with Developmentally Disabled Persons. Hershey: Pennsylvania State University College of Medicine.

Hoveland, C. I., I. L. Janis, and H. H. Kelley (1953) Communications and Persuasion. New Haven, CT: Yale University Press.

Kahn, Robert L., Donald M. Wolfe, Robert P. Quinn, and Diedrick Snoek (1964) Organizational Stress: Studies in Role Conflict and Ambiguity. New York: John Wiley.

Kalleberg, Arne L. (1977) "Work values and job rewards: a theory of job satisfaction." American Sociological Review 42:124-143.

Katz, Daniel and Robert L. Kahn (1966) The Social Psychology of Organizations. New York: John Wiley.

Kazdin, Alan E. (1977) The Token Economy: A Review and Evaluation. New York: Plenum.

Kelman, Herbert C. and Donald P. Warwick (1973) "Bridging micro and macro approaches to social change: a social-psychological perspective," pp. 13-59 in G. Zaltman (ed.) Processes and Phenomena of Social Change. New York: John Wiley.

Kiesler, Charles A., Barry E. Collins, and Norman Miller (1969) Attitude Change: A Critical Analysis of Theoretical Positions. New York: John Wiley.

Kunkel, John H. (1975) Behavior, Social Problems, and Change: A Social Learning Approach. Englewood Cliffs, NJ: Prentice-Hall.

Lawler, Edward E. (1976) "Control systems in organizations," pp. 1247-1291 in Marvin D. Dunnette (ed.) Handbook of Industrial and Organizational Psychology. Chicago: Rand McNally.

Leithwood, Kenneth A. and Deborah A. Montgomery (1980) "Evaluating program implementation." Evaluation Review 4:193-214.

Levine, Robert A. (1972) Public Planning: Failure & Redirection. New York: Basic Books.

Lewin, Kurt (1947) "Frontiers in group dynamics." Human Relations 1:2-38.

Lin, Nan and Gerald Zaltman (1973) "Dimensions of innovations," pp. 93-115 in G. Zaltman (ed.) Processes and Phenomena of Social Change. New York: John Wiley.

Loucks, Susan F., and Marge Melle (1980) "Implementation of a district-wide science curriculum: the effects of a three-year effort." Presented at the American Educational Research Association Annual Meeting, Boston, April 1980.

Loucks, Susan F., Beulah W. Newlove, and Gene E. Hall (1975) Measuring Levels of Use of the Innovation: A Manual for Trainers, Interviewers, and Raters. Austin: Research and Development Center for Teacher Education, University of Texas.

Lukas, Carol V. (1975) "Problems in implementing Head Start Planned Variation models," pp. 113-125 in A. Rivlin and P. M. Timpane (eds.) Planned Variation in Education: Should We Give Up or Try Harder? Washington, DC: Brookings.

McLaughlin, M. (1976) "Implementation as mutual adaptation: change in classroom organization," pp. 167-180 in W. Williams and R. F. Elmore (eds.) Social Program Implementation. New York: Academic Press.

March, James G. and Herbert A. Simon (1958) Organizations. New York: John Wiley.

Melcher, Arlyn J. (1976) Structure and Process of Organizations: A Systems Approach. Englewood Cliffs, NJ: Prentice-Hall.

Miles, Robert H. and William D. Perreault, Jr. (1976) "Organizational role conflict: its antecedents and consequences." Organizational Behavior and Human Performance 17:19-44.

Milio, Nancy (1971) "Health care organizations and innovation." Journal of Health and Social Behavior 12:163-173.

Murphy, Jerome T. (1976) "Title V of ESEA: the impact of discretionary funds on state education bureaucracies," pp. 77-100 in W. Williams and R. F. Elmore (eds.) Social Program Implementation. New York: Academic Press.

Nunnally, J. C. (1967) Psychometric Theory. New York: McGraw-Hill.

Patton, Michael Q. (1979) "Evaluation of program implementation," pp. 318-346 in L. Sechrest (ed.) Evaluation Studies Review Annual, Vol. 4. Beverly Hills, CA: Sage.

Pincus, John (1974) "Incentives for innovation in the public schools." Review of Educational Research 44:113-144.

Pressman, Jeffrey L. and Aaron Wildavsky (1973) Implementation. Berkeley: University of California Press.

Quilitch, H. Robert (1975) "A comparison of three staff management procedures." Journal of Applied Behavior Analysis 8:59-66.

Quinn, Robert P., Graham L. Staines, and Margaret R. McCullough (1974) Job Satisfaction: Is There a Trend? Manpower Research Monograph No. 30. Washington, DC: U.S. Department of Labor.

Radnor, Michael, Irwin Feller, and Everett Rogers (1978) The Diffusion of Innovations: An Assessment. Evanston, IL: Northwestern University Center for the Interdisciplinary Study of Science and Technology.

Rappaport, Julian, Jack M. Chinsky, and Emory L. Cowen (1971) Innovations in Helping Chronic Patients: College Students in a Mental Institution. New York: Academic Press.

Rivlin, Alice M. and P. Michael Timpane [eds.] (1975) Planned Variation in Education: Should We Give Up or Try Harder? Washington, DC: Brookings.

Rizzo, John R., Robert J. House, and Sidney I. Lirtzman (1970) "Role conflict and ambiguity in complex organizations." Administrative Science Quarterly 15:150-163.

Roethlisberger, Fritz J. and William J. Dickson (1939) Management and the Worker. Cambridge, MA: Harvard University Press.

Rogers, David L. and Joseph Molnar (1976) "Organizational antecedents of role conflict and ambiguity in top level administrators." Administrative Science Quarterly 21:598-610.

Rogers, Everett M. and F. F. Shoemaker (1971) Communication of Innovations. New York: Free Press.

Rosenberg, Nathan (1978) "The diffusion of technology: an economic historian's view," pp. 19-40 in M. Radnor, I. Feller, and E. Rogers (eds.) The Diffusion of Innovations: An Assessment. Evanston, IL: Northwestern University Center for the Interdisciplinary Study of Science and Technology.

Rosenthal, R. and L. Jacobson (1968) Pygmalion in the Classroom. New York: Holt, Rinehart & Winston.

Rossi, Peter H., Howard E. Freeman, and Sonia R. Wright (1979) Evaluation: A Systematic Approach. Beverly Hills, CA: Sage.

Rothman, Jack (1974) Planning and Organizing for Social Change: Action Principles from Social Science Research. New York: Columbia University Press.

Sabatier, Paul and Daniel Mazmanian (1980) "The implementation of public policy: a framework of analysis." Policy Studies Journal 8:538-560.

——— (1979) "The conditions of effective implementation: a guide to accomplishing policy objectives." Policy Analysis 5: 481-504.

Sarasen, Seymour B. (1972) The Creation of Settings and the Future Societies. San Francisco: Jossey-Bass.

Scheff, Thomas (1961) "Control over policy by attendants in a mental hospital." Journal of Health & Human Behavior 2:93-105.

Schmuck, Richard A. and Matthew B. Miles (1971) Organizational Development in Schools. Palo Alto, CA: National Press Books.

Schulman, Jay (1969) Remaking an Organization: Innovation in a Specialized Psychiatric Hospital. Albany: State University of New York Press.

Schuman, Howard and M. P. Johnson (1976) "Attitudes and behavior," pp. 161-207 in Alex Inkeles, James Coleman, and Neil Smelser (eds.) Annual Review of Sociology, Vol. 2. Palo Alto, CA: Annual Reviews.

Sechrest, Lee and Robin Rednor (1979) "Strenth and integrity of treatments in evaluation studies." Florida State University. (unpublished)

Smith, Clagett G. and James A. King (1975) Mental Hospitals: A Study in Organizational Effectiveness. Lexington, MA: D. C. Heath.

Smith, Louis M. and Pat M. Keith (1971) Anatomy of Educational Innovation: An Organizational Analysis of an Elementary School. New York: John Wiley.

Smith, Patricia Cain, Lorne M. Kendall, and Charles L. Hulin (1969) The Measurement of Satisfaction in Work and Retirement: A Strategy for the Study of Attitudes. Chicago: Rand McNally.

Stinchcomb, Arthur L. (1965) "Social structure and organizations," pp. 142-193 in James G. March (ed.) Handbook of Organizations. Chicago: Rand McNally.

Thompson, James D. (1967) Organizations in Action: Social Science Bases of Administrative Theory. New York: McGraw-Hill.

Tornatzky, Louis G., Esther O. Fergus, Joseph W. Avellar, George W. Fairweather, and Mitchell Fleischer (1980) Innovation and Social Process: A National Experiment in Implementing Social Technology. Elmsford, NY: Pergamon.

Warwick, Donald P. (1975) A Theory of Public Bureaucracy: Politics, Personality and Organization in the State Department. Cambridge, MA: Harvard University Press.

Watson, Goodwin (1973) "Resistance to change," pp. 117-131 in G. Zaltman (ed.) Processes and Phenomena of Social Change. New York: John Wiley.

Weatherley, Richard and Michael Lipsky (1977) "Street-level bureaucrats and institutional innovation: implementing special education reform." Harvard Educational Review 47:171-197.

Weikert, David P. and Bernard A. Banet (1976) "Planned variation from the perspective of a model sponsor," pp. 125-148 in W. Williams and R. F. Elmore (eds.) Social Program Implementation. New York: Academic Press.

――― (1975) "Model design problems in Follow Through," pp. 61-77 in Alice Rivlin and P. Michael Timpane (eds.) Planned Variation in Education: Should We Give Up or Try Harder? Washington, DC: Brookings.

Wilkinson, Gregg (1973) "Interaction patterns and staff response to psychiatric innovations." Journal of Health & Social Behavior 14: 323-329.

Williams, Walter (1980) The Implementation Perspective. Berkeley: University of California Press.

――― (1976a) "Introduction," pp. 3-14 in W. Williams and R. F. Elmore (eds.) Social Program Implementation. New York: Academic Press.

――― (1976b) "Implementation problems in federally funded programs," pp. 15-40 in W. Williams and R. F. Elmore (eds.) Social Program Implementation. New York: Academic Press.

――― (1976c) "Implementation analysis and assessment," pp. 267-282 in W. Williams and R. F. Elmore (eds.) Social Program Implementation. New York: Academic Press.

――― and Richard F. Elmore [eds.] (1976) Social Program Implementation. New York: Academic Press.

Yin, Robert K. (1979) Changing Urban Bureaucracies: How New Practices Become Routinized. Lexington, MA: D. C. Heath.

Zand, D. E. and R. E. Sorensen (1975) "Theory of change and the effective use of management science." Administrative Science Quarterly 20:532-545.

About the Author

Mary Ann Scheirer is an applied social psychologist emphasizing the integration of process analysis into evaluation research. After completing her doctorate in sociology at Cornell University, she was an evaluation specialist at the U.S. Office of Education before joining JWK International Corporation of Annandale, Virginia as a Senior Research Associate.

Previous evaluation research projects have examined open classroom elementary education, the Follow Through compensatory education program, the use of nurse practitioners in nursing education, and the monitoring of Medicaid/Medicare provider facilities. Dr. Scheirer's current research includes quantitative analysis of welfare costs related to teenage motherhood. She is continuing the research reported in this book by intensively examining techniques for the measurement of implementation.